The Himalayan Shuffle

The
Himalayan
Shuffle

Edward Ley-Wilson

Lochar Publishing · Moffat · Scotland

© Edward Ley-Wilson 1992

Published by Lochar Publishing Ltd,
MOFFAT, SCOTLAND, DG10 9ED.

A catalogue record for this book is available from the British Library

ISBN 1 874027 33 1

Design and Production by Jeff A Peers, Impressive Graphics.

Typeset in 10.5pt on 13pt Meridien by The Word Shop

Printed in Great Britain by
Billing & Sons Ltd, Worcester

*To my wife Leah, whose care, patience, enthusiasm and
ability to suffer my ever-changing moods
makes it all possible.*

CONTENTS

Foreword

In 1988, entirely self supported, Edward Ley-Wilson and his partner had the adventure of a lifetime having experienced remotest China as few have ever done. They ran 1200 miles of the 1800 miles length of the Wall before their sixth arrest by the Chinese authorities forced them to return home.

This feeling of leaving a journey incomplete is something I have experienced a number of times on attempts to walk unsupported to the North Pole. It serves only to make one try harder the next time.

Due to growing political difficulties in China, another attempt at the Great Wall became increasingly unlikely and thus "The Himalayan Shuffle" was born.

Edward Ley-Wilson and Justin Mattersons' self contained run across the entire length of the Himalayas was a magnificent undertaking and a remarkable achievement, made more so when considering the distances covered and the nature of the terrain. Their story is a triumph of sporting endeavour and an example to all of low cost, minimum impact and modern day adventuring. I feel proud to have been associated with them.

RANULPH FIENNES

Acknowledgements

A journey like this crosses international boundaries and areas usually closed to foreigners. For their help in creating the paperwork that made it all possible I must thank:

Wasim Zaman, who found time for us in a busy schedule; Mr Jha and Miss Gulati of the Indian Home Ministry in New Delhi; Mr Badri Khanal at the Nepalese Embassy in London; Mr Adrian Stones at the British Embassy in New Delhi; Mr D.N. Saraf in New Delhi; Mark Tully, BBC Correspondent in New Delhi; Holly and Pablo Segovia in Kathmandu; and Mr Singh of the Nepali Immigration office for smoothing the permit applications.

Thanks also to Reebok UK for their continued support; to Mountain Equipment; United Biscuits Chilled Foods (Luton) and Prontaprint (Luton); Andrew Dunsmore for driving for four hours in the rain; Mark Waltham of I.T. in Kathmandu for putting up with the smell; and Caroline Whitfield of Ideas Inc. in London.

I must also mention innumerable friends whose support and good humour buoyed me up when it looked as if it was all going wrong. In particular, David Wightman of 'China Wall Run '88' fame; David Hubbard, fell-running partner extraordinaire; Philippa Baker for her Triathlon; and my parents and parents-in-law for spreading the word.

Finally, sincere thanks must go to Sir Ranulph Fiennes, whose patronage was an invaluable asset, and to John Ridgway for his inspiration in years past.

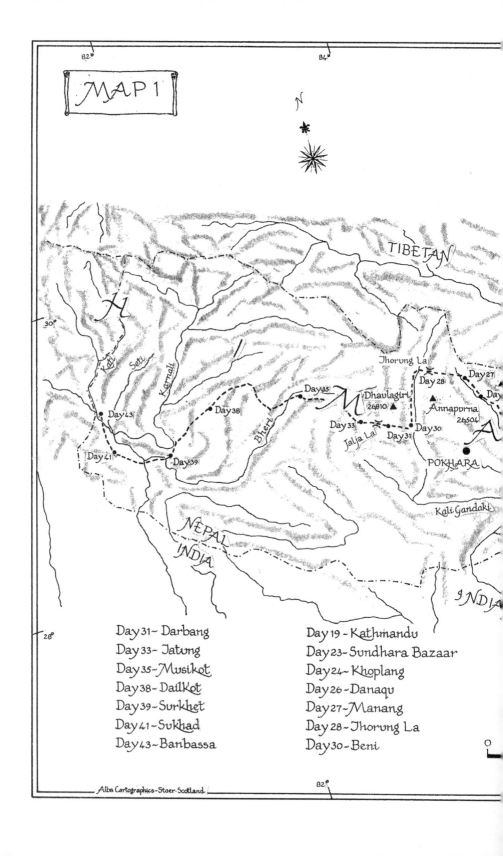

82°

84°

MAP 1

N

TIBETAN

30°

Seti

Karnali

Bheri

Thorung La

Day 28

Day 27

Day

Day 35

Dhaulagiri
26810 ▲

Annapurna
26504 ▲

Day 43

Day 38

Day 33

Day 31

Day 30

Jalja La

Day 21

Day 39

POKHARA

Kali Gandaki

NEPAL

INDIA

INDIA

28°

82°

Day 31~ Darbang
Day 33~ Jatung
Day 35~ Musikot
Day 38~ Dailkot
Day 39~ Surkhet
Day 41~ Sukhad
Day 43~ Banbassa

Day 19 ~ Kathmandu
Day 23~ Sundhara Bazaar
Day 24~ Khoplang
Day 26~ Danaqu
Day 27~ Manang
Day 28 ~ Thorung La
Day 30~ Beni

Alba Cartographics-Stoer-Scotland

82°

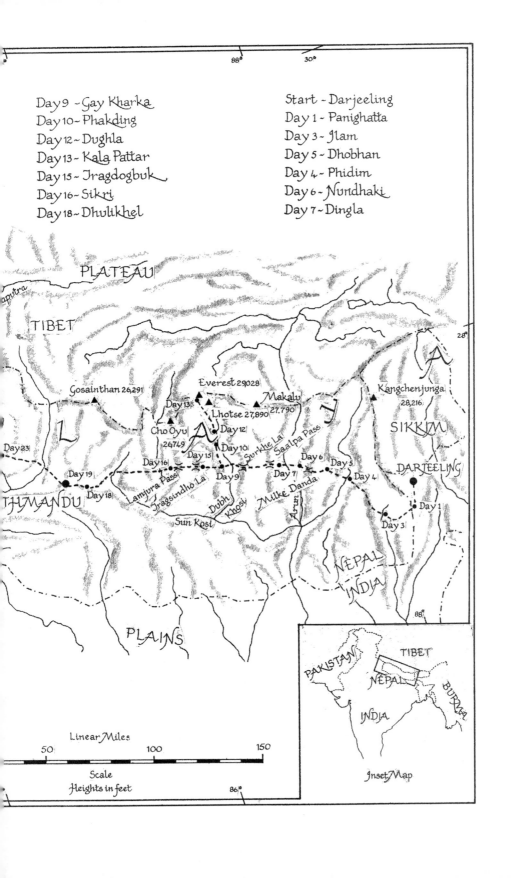

Day 9 - Gay Kharka
Day 10 - Phakding
Day 12 - Dughla
Day 13 - Kala Pattar
Day 15 - Iragdogbuk
Day 16 - Sikri
Day 18 - Dhulikhel

Start - Darjeeling
Day 1 - Panighatta
Day 3 - Ilam
Day 5 - Dhobhan
Day 4 - Phidim
Day 6 - Nundhaki
Day 7 - Dingla

PLATEAU

TIBET

Gosainthan 26,291

Everest 29,028

Makalu 27,790

Kangchenjunga 28,216

Day 13

Lhotse 27,890

Cho Oyu 26,749

SIKKIM

Surkhe La

Saalpa Pass

Day 12

Day 23

Day 10

DARJEELING

Day 16

Day 15

Day 6

Day 5

KHMANDU

Day 19

Day 18

Lamjura Pass

Iragsindho La

Day 9

Day 7

Day 4

Dudh Khosi

Sun Kosi

Milke Danda

Arun

Day 1

Day 3

NEPAL

INDIA

PLAINS

PAKISTAN

TIBET

NEPAL

BURMA

INDIA

Inset Map

Linear Miles
50   100   150
Scale
Heights in feet

'Still, as addictive drugs go, if body building is
say cocaine, and golf is Maltesers, then running is
a cocktail of heroin, crack and ecstasy, with a
sprinkling of angel dust for good measure. The
whole lot bubbled through a suspension of coal gas
in paint solvent and injected straight into the
carotid artery with a grease gun.'
Andy Blackford

Chapter 1

A SCREW LOOSE

'I want to marry you, will you have me?' A moment's stunned silence, then her reaction told me that she would. Leah was to be my wife at last. We were sitting in the green, grassy knoll below the summit of Snowdon. The sun blazed from a blue sky, and glittered wetly off the Welsh Llyns far below, a pair of ravens wheeled and dived in the warm breeze and all around the Welsh mountains filled our eyes with grandeur.

When we had finally let go of each other I said, 'There's something else.' My voice faltered.

Leah looked questioningly up at me with those huge, brown, doe eyes of hers and I thought to myself, Oh God, I'm about to ruin a great day.

'Go on then,' she said.

'I'm going to run the Himalayas.'

'Before or after the wedding?' came the instant reply.

'After. Quite a long time after.'

'And how long will you be gone this time?' She was used to my disappearing off to far flung places for months at a time.

'Four months.' The tiny muscles in her cheeks quivered ever so slightly.

'Who's going with you?'

'I don't know yet, maybe Dave would come.' Dave Wightman had been my partner on a running expedition to China in 1988.

'And is it dangerous?' Those doe eyes again.

'Only if I don't prepare properly beforehand.'

The silence fell on us and she turned away to look out east over the hills of upland Wales. On the other side of the valley tiny figures balanced precariously on the knife-edge ridge of Crib Goch and, far away, Tryfan and the windswept Glyders glowed a hazy grey in the summer sun.

'Will you still marry me?' It was an unfair question and I knew it.

'Only if you promise to come back alive. I'm too young to be a widow.' That mischievous look told me all I needed to know.

We were married on 24 September 1988 and I was to leave for the Himalayas sixteen months later. When the time came to leave, Leah had taken on the charity fund raising *in toto* and had become the expedition coordinator responsible for ensuring the right thing happened at the right time. I had the easy job. All I had to do was run.

The idea to run the Himalayas was born in a grotty little police station in China in 1988. Dave Wightman and I had run for 1,200 miles along the Great Wall and had been arrested six times for our pains. This was the sixth arrest. I put my head back against the dirty grey wall of the Chinese police inspector's office and thought over the trip. It had certainly been exciting: running and hiding from the Chinese police, being interrogated and fined, and some great running over dry and barren northern China. But something was missing and I knew now what it was. The challenge and satisfaction of travelling under our own steam from A to B without a break in the journey had been denied us. The arrests had turned our run into a stop-start affair, and the burden of leaving something incomplete lay heavy on my shoulders. I sat there, listening to Dave trying to persuade the policeman that we were not spies and dreamed of where I could run to next.

It would be a mountain run of course, something hard, something to test mind and spirit a little, and it would have to be somewhere I had not already been. But most of all, it had to be somewhere free, somewhere where policemen didn't exist, where the effort could be a continuous one, unhindered by politics and petty officialdom. The Andes maybe? How about running the length of Chile, or the Rockies. Canada is a free country; I wouldn't get any trouble there. The Alps, the Pyrenees, the Atlas mountains. I know . . . the Himalayas. The greatest mountain range on earth. They pass through Nepal and India; no problems there surely. They house fourteen of the world's greatest mountains. All fourteen are over 26,000 feet. Everest, Goddess Mother of the Earth, Kanjenjunga, Annapurna, K2, Nanga Parbat to name but a few. Yes, the Himalayas, it had to be. I could traverse all fourteen peaks. That would make for a fascinating 2,000-mile journey, filled with mountain running and with opportunities to experience the myriad of different cultures and traditions of the people living there.

'The Himalayas, Dave, that's the next one.'

'What was that?' He looked up from his urgent discussions with the policeman. His face was streaked with sweat and a ten-day beard blackened his chin. His clothes were brown with the dust and dirt of the run and he looked knackered. I was in the same boat.

'The Himalayas. I'm going to run the Himalayas next.'

'Bloody hell, Ed. I'm engaged in desperate negotiations with these guys, trying to prevent them from shooting us as spies and all you can think about is, "what next?"' The urgent discussion with the policeman was resumed. I closed my eyes, mouthed softly to myself, 'Running the Himalayas. Perfect,' and began to plan.

One year after Dave and I had returned to Britain, on a cold and blowy May evening in 1989, I rang him at his home in Peterborough. We were by now well over the aftermath of our China trip and had both been working hard in new jobs. I was in the food industry as a training man and Dave was buying machinery in the printing world. He was just getting over a painful knee operation and would not be able to run for many months. He had obviously forgotten our little exchange in that cold grey police station in northern China.

'You're going to do what? My suspicions are confirmed, matey. You've got a screw loose, I always knew it. Why can't you take a nice, relaxing, comfortable, beach holiday in the French Riviera for once?'

'Yes, well, thanks for the advice, old chap. It's great to have your support.'

'It's a pleasure. I suppose you want me to look after that delicious wife of yours while you're away.'

'If you don't mind.'

'Of course I don't mind. Maybe I'll finish up that old bottle of whisky as well. Now, don't go getting involved with any marauding Yetis; don't take your socks off inside; and remember, eat with your right and wipe with your left.'

'You're a good man . . . I think.'

'Yes, well, just make sure you come back in one piece. Your wife's too young to be a widow.'

'Someone else I know told me that as well. Listen Dave, this run has become very important to me and whatever happens, I'm giving it all I've got. I'm just sorry we're not going together this time.'

'So am I, matey. Maybe next time, uh?'

'Yes, maybe next time.'

By now, home in our little Luton flat (which Leah and I had bought in 1988 just as the property market reached its peak and were now trying to sell as the same market wallowed in its trough of high interest rates), the paperwork had started to mount up. There was so much to do and, as always, so little time to do it.

Leah at home as the paperwork starts to pile up

Special permission for the run to follow my chosen route was required from both the Indian and Nepalese governments; kit had to be chosen and purchased (or donated); expedition brochures were compiled and posted to hundreds of potential sponsors; letters were sent all over the globe; expensive telephone calls were made to the USA and to India; and still on top of all this I had to find time for a daily ten-mile run. Our jobs took up all weekdays, so all this frantic activity took place in the dark of the early morning or the evening. There was paper everywhere: in the living room, the bedroom, the kitchen and the tiny hall. Our little flat was a mass of scribbled notes, letters to be posted, kit and smelly running socks, as the training and preparation intensified.

But how to choose a partner? That was the tricky one. I could count potential partners on the fingers of one hand. I needed someone I could trust, someone who could afford to take four months off and someone who was physically and mentally capable of taking on the task. The obvious choice was my good friend Dave Wightman of 'China Wall Run' fame but his knee injury, brought on by our efforts in China the year before, put paid to this partnership. Added to that was the fact that he had just started in a new job, so a four-month break at this time would not have done him any favours.

Then another name swam into view. What about Justin Matterson? Of course, he would be ideal. I had first met Justin five years before when we worked together at an Outward Bound Centre in Scotland. When the working season came to an end we found ourselves flung together again with the Ridgway family on an expedition into remotest Peru. Justin was a man who loved a challenge and had the physical and mental endurance to take on the Himalayas. Born into a wealthy family, he had wanted for little for most of his twenty-seven years and after a time in the family business, had shunned the conventional world and taken to the seas. For the last four years, he had been crewing and skippering yachts of all shapes and sizes in some of the most dangerous waters anywhere in the world. When he wasn't sailing he was helping to run Outward Bound courses, an activity which kept him fit. I remembered him as a quiet, self-conscious, rather awkward chap, who nonetheless had a thirst for adventure and an ability to keep going, come what may. I wrote him a letter.

By return of post, I had a partner.

Chapter 2

NEVER THE TWAIN SHALL MEET

Things began to move at lightning speed. Justin and I met and talked and ran and got to know each other again; the kit started to arrive through the door; Reebok came up trumps and supplied us each with four pairs of shoes and full Gore-Tex rain suits; Justin dashed around London finding us, amongst other things, better socks, UV sunglasses and full medical kit; I spent a small fortune on train fares, travelling up and down from Luton to London, visiting embassies and chivvying sloth-like officials to give us full permission for the run; and Sir Ranulph Fiennes agreed to become the expedition's patron.

Sir Ranulph had also been the patron of the expedition to run the Great Wall of China in 1988. Both the China Wall and the Himalayan trips were exercises in self-sufficiency, and his recent attempts to walk, unsupported, to the North Pole, accorded with my own attitude to expeditioning. Self-sufficiency was the name of the game. To move across rough and difficult terrain entirely under your own power. To me there is something wonderfully pure in the concept of being a self-contained unit, of being quite on your own, of being able to change plans as you go along, of not being bound by any schedules or responsibilities other than those of the aims of the expedition. Justin and I would have no back-up team, no Land Rovers to meet us once a week. We would live each day as it came, carry the bare minimum of kit and take a chance on food and water being available. As we saw it, we only needed to come across one homestead per day in order to get enough food, and we could drink from the mountain streams. Our kit would cope with conditions down to fifteen degrees below zero if we had to sleep out and, well, it wasn't meant to be easy anyway. We had just one rule, and that was that we would keep going each day until we came across something. My experiences in China told me that when you're covering twenty-five to forty miles a day, the landscape shrinks and as long as you just keep going, you will eventually get somewhere.

The opportunity to raise money for a charity from our run was irresistible and we searched around for a group whose approach to Third World poverty was in keeping with our own views on self-sufficiency. The Intermediate Technology Development Group then entered our lives. We chose I.T. because their whole ethic revolves around helping people in the Third World help themselves.

Donning pinstripe suits, we put the idea to them at their office in Rugby and after they had chewed it around for a while, we got a positive answer. The aims of the expedition were now set: to run the length of the Himalayas and to raise money for Intermediate Technology. We were in business!

Justin and I pored over maps galore and worked out a route. The aim was to traverse all fourteen of the highest peaks of the Himalayas. Starting in Darjeeling in north-east India, we would cross into Nepal, then run north-west across the grain of the land, aiming for Kala Pattar, the hill overlooking Everest Base Camp. This would be the highest point of the trip at 17,900 feet. From here we would attempt the 250-mile dash to Kathmandu, where we would pick up more kit. Then westwards, through the ancient capital of Gorkha, cutting north up and round the Annapurna Massif to cross the Thorong La (pass) at 17,300 feet, and down the deepest valley in the world, the Kali Gandaki. A traverse of remote western Nepal would follow, before we crossed the border into India. Special permission to cross this border was needed from the Indian government. Then we would head for the Indian Himalayas, where the cultural and religious differences would be most marked, through Uttar Pradesh and Himachal Pradesh, and finally into Kashmir, jewel of the East, to finish at Gulmarg, high above the Kashmir Valley.

This route marked a true traverse east to west of the fourteen major peaks from Kanjenjunga to Nanga Parbat. Our measurements showed it to be approximately 2,000 miles, though it is impossible to be exact, for the map simply cannot show the thousands of squiggles in the path nor the ups and downs. The route on the ground, therefore, would be considerably longer, but as the map said 2,000 miles, we could only claim 2,000. Our target was one hundred days, but both of us secretly thought this was quite impossible. There were two detours in the route, one up to the base of Mount Everest and the other round the Annapurna Massif, but both were quite irresistible.

I had been running all year and had just changed the nature of my training to suit the coming challenge. I spent more and more time out on the hills and mountains of Britain, putting in long, hard days. Leah was as long-suffering, uncomplaining and supportive as ever. Driving north on a Saturday, having risen at three o'clock in the morning, she would dump me at the foot of some cold and windswept mountain in Wales or the Lake District. I'd do my warm-up exercises by the car, wave goodbye, then disappear upwards into the mist and the hills for the rest of the day. I loved these days on my own, pushing my body to its limit, revelling in a new-found endurance. I would go on all day, sometimes without stopping at all, my legs just eating up the ground. Then, as the evening light painted the hills pink then blue then grey, I would plunge down off the tops to arrive tired, wet, muddy and sore at the car, where Leah would prop me up with Mars bars and mugs of hot tea from the Thermos. Sometimes my runs took longer. I entered the Karrimor International Mountain Marathon for October 1989. This was to be a final test of my fitness before I left for the Himalayas. The KIMM, as it is affectionately known, is the most gruelling mountain race in the calendar. Two days of orienteering in difficult terrain, under the clock. Thirty miles and 9,000 feet of climbing on the first day, an overnight camp (always in the rain), then twenty miles and 6,000 feet of climbing on the second day. As my partner and I set off on Day One, the stormclouds were already gathering and the wind freshening from the south-west.

By the end of Day One, over half of the pairs in our class had given up and by the start of Day Two another ten pairs had had second thoughts during the night. By the time we had run two-thirds of Day Two my partner's ankle had given way completely and we too had to retire. But despite this early finish, I felt great. My running was good and strong right to the end and I knew my training had worked. I was ready to go.

Christmas and New Year passed in a blur of money-raising, kit-checking, visa-stamping and publicity-posing. I tied up every-thing at work and left. Then suddenly February arrived and it was time to fly.

At the airport, we queued with others heading out to the Far

East. Our little backpacks and two small bags of spare kit looked minuscule compared to the mass of trunks and suitcases that was our fellow travellers' luggage. But we didn't care, we were on a high. A large group of family and friends had come to see us off, and after lasting goodbyes and good lucks, we waved a final farewell and disappeared through into the departure lounge. We were off at last.

On the plane I found it hard to relax. I felt fit and raring to go. What would we find, would we get permission, when would we start running, how could we drop the extra kit off . . .? All these questions and more raced around inside my head. I had lived and breathed this expedition for nearly two years and I was keen to get things organised as soon as possible. I sat there with a big grin on my face, happy that we were on our way. But despite my good mood, I had a worry. I still felt ill at ease with my partner.

Justin and I were two different kinds of people, there was no getting away from that fact. We had had quite different upbringings and had met only briefly when we worked together in Scotland for six months in 1985. Then, we had found each other impossible to live with. Our views on life, the way we went about things, what we liked and disliked, all these things were entirely different.

Yet here we were, setting off on the greatest adventure of our lives and attempting something as ridiculously difficult as running the entire length of the Himalayas. I was excited, yet my enthusiasm dulled slightly as we finally found ourselves alone together on the aeroplane. I was going to share my life with this guy for the next four months. He would need me and I would need him. But would we survive as a partnership? It was five years since we had worked grudgingly together in Scotland. Five years since we had travelled together with the Ridgway family in the remote highlands of South America. Then, the emotional strain of being flung together in some extremely dangerous situations had been too much. We were at each other's throats nearly every day and were unable to agree on anything. The degree of effort we would each have to expend on this expedition would far outweigh our experiences in South America and I wondered whether the immense emotional and physical strains that we were about to inflict on ourselves would break us. Would all this ancient animosity rear its ugly head again? Inside, I longed to say what I felt, but I kept quiet. I was the originator of this expedition and I had asked Justin to come with me. It was therefore my responsibility to keep us together, to keep us moving forward, for despite our personal differences, we now had a common goal and each of us needed the other to achieve it. It was time to push any animosity to the back of my mind and concentrate on keeping the two of us together. I resolved to be as professional as possible in my attitude towards my partner and, in this situation, that meant a need for patience and tact, neither of which I was renowned for. It would be a good test.

From the outside, we seemed quite a good potential partnership. Both of us had some experience of the wilder parts of our planet; both had been in positions of responsibility when danger reared its head and had had to deal with it; and both of us had lived closely together with other people before. I would supply the drive and Justin would supply the brakes. Both would be needed if we were to achieve our target of one hundred days. Yes indeed, on the outside we should be a good team. But right now, winging our way east at 550 miles per hour, we were cagey and suspicious of each other.

Chapter 3

YOU MUST BE PATIENT AND PERSISTENT

Delhi: thirty degrees Celsius, hot and sticky and bustling with life. Built up in the 1920s, it is the seat of the Indian government and, in the grand Parliament Buildings, decisions are made that affect the multitude who make up the second most populous nation on earth. The streets are wide and dusty, and the dust creates a permanent haze as it hangs in the sticky heat like smoke.

We checked into the Yadri Niwas Hotel, a Russian-built, drab, concrete, eighteen-storey nightmare. I'm sure it is a converted KGB prison. With its dark corridors, concrete rooms and open liftshafts, a man could disappear forever inside here and no-one would know. In our room, the bed is a raised concrete platform with two thin mattresses. There is a shower, two bedside lights, a mosquito screen and a hot water tap, none of which work, but it's a base and it's cheap.

We needed to sleep off the flight for a couple of hours and the last thing I saw before I closed my eyes was the vultures perched in the trees opposite our window. 'Wake me if they come knocking,' said Justin and slept.

That afternoon we started to get things organised. I was to set about getting permission for the run and Justin was to organise the kit drop-offs. Both took a full week.

I followed leads and contacts, first arranged back in England. My wife belongs to an enormous family, who are spread out all over the world, and it was my father-in-law, Qamruz Zaman, whose family hail from Bangladesh, who helped to set the ball rolling. Qamruz put me onto his brother, who works for the United Nations. From his base in New York, Wasim Zaman organises aid in its many and varied forms for the Third World, specifically India,

Pakistan, Nepal and Bangladesh. Now, he has a sister, whose husband is a dentist, who pulls the teeth of the Nepalese ex-Ambassador to Bangladesh, who knows the Home Minister in Kathmandu, who can give us the permission we need on the Nepalese side. It's a long shot, but it's a lead. In India, I was advised to telephone a Mr Saraf, ex-minister for handicrafts, and pick up what leads I could from there.

Rickety cabs, black and yellow, ply the avenues for trade. Covered scooter tricycles, full to the gunnels with passengers, dodge and weave as they vie for road space; tired-looking cyclists pedal warily down the sides of the road; a sign on the back of a bus says, 'Don't kiss me too nearly'; and on the sidewalks people walk and talk and buy and sell with a fervour that only the Indians could manage in this heat. Everyone wears flat, open sandals or flipflops; there are loosely hanging robes, *saris*, cheap trousers and jackets; men with turbans and full beards topped with fantastic 'twiddled' moustaches; ladies with intricate nose rings; lepers sitting on the road, rotting limbs displayed for a few coins and tiny, dirty, barefoot children playing in the dust.

Mr Saraf was a neat, wrinkled gentleman with a twinkle in his eye and a permanent half-smile on his lips. He was dressed in an immaculate Nehru suit, his dark grey hair carefully combed to cover a balding patch. We sat and drank tea from tiny glasses and ate dry toast. I explained what I was trying to do.

'You must be very patient,' he advised. 'Yes, patient and persistent if you want to get permission. This is what I suggest you do.' He then scribbled down some names and telephone numbers of government officials. I had my second lead.

The rest of the week was spent dashing from one government office to another until at last Miss Gulati and Mr Jha of the Home Ministry came up trumps with a letter fully authorising the expedition and allowing us to pass through the closed western Nepalese/Indian border. The catalyst that moved them into action was not the mass of references, expedition brochures, route maps, etc. in which I had drowned them, but a single *Daily Telegraph* article outlining the run. Once they had seen the article, I was a celebrity in their eyes and permission was quickly forthcoming. I have Andrew Dunsmore, professional photographer and friend, to thank for that. I burst back into the hotel room, the permission papers clutched in my sweaty palm, and whooped with joy.

Nothing could stop us now.

Justin too was having success, but not without a struggle. Sending a parcel in India is an experience definitely to be avoided if at all possible. You stroll along in the heat with your package to the Post Office. They tell you to come back with it wrapped in white cloth. Rather bewildered, you disappear off again to find the cloth. The market is the only place you can buy it and that is half an hour's walk away. You buy the cloth, wrap the parcel, tie it with string and return to the Post Office. You are then told that string is no good, you must sew it up and then use red wax. You lose your temper and start to sweat. Where to get red wax? In the market . . . bloody hell! Storm off, buy a red candle, sew the cloth, drip the wax, storm back, and find the Post Office has closed for lunch. Sit outside in a filthy temper, sweating buckets. One hour later the Post Office opens. Stand in the queue for another hour, fill in forms, pay and post the parcel. Never again.

He eventually had to drop one of the parcels off himself, which meant an overnight bus journey up to Manali in the Indian Himalayas.

While he set off on his 'Manali-drop-the-kit-off-and-jump-straight-back-on-the-bus' trip, I donned shirt and borrowed tie and jet-setted over to an Embassy party, by special invitation. People from Britain, Russia, Pakistan, Malaysia, India, Finland and Australia. All were exchanging cards and flitting from one introduction to another. So while Justin was sitting on a draughty, rickety, bouncing old bus in the dark, I was lording it with the world's diplomats and drinking G and Ts. Did I feel guilty? Did I heck!

Just before we left for Kathmandu and Nepal we went to see Adrian Stones, Second Secretary for Information at the British High Commission in Delhi. We needed to know more about the growing unrest in the north-western state of Kashmir. Even before we left England the headlines told their own story:

War clouds gather over Kashmir.
Hindu hardliners urge crackdown on Muslims.
Detailed proof of Pakistan hand in Jammu and Kashmir.

This was not what we needed. Our run was due to finish in Kashmir, and it was now touch-and-go as to whether or not we would be able to get through. Our letter of permission also included entry into Kashmir, but if India and Pakistan were slogging hell out of each other by the time we got there, it was unlikely we would be able to complete our journey.

India and Pakistan have already been to war over Kashmir three times since partition, in 1947, 1965 and 1972. Each time India has won, but the underlying problems of this sensitive border state still remain. Kashmir is sixty per cent Muslim while the rest of India, including the government, is predominantly Hindu. Kashmir has suffered from lack of investment in industry and education and therefore the standard of living, compared to other parts of India, is poor.

The Kashmiri people are a proud race too and have survived as a princely state even under British rule. Now, their country is split in two. Pakistan occupies the northern part and India the southern. A 'cease-fire line' separates the two.

Right now the Indian army was sitting in the Kashmir valley in force. Twenty-four-hour curfews were being imposed, foreign journalists were being thrown out of the state and people were being killed on the streets of Srinagar, the capital, every day. The situation did not look too good.

One newspaper report stated that Pakistan, in its desire to support the Kashmiri uprising, might use its nuclear weapons as a last resort.

At the British High Commission Adrian Stones met us in his air-conditioned office. Upright, in his thirties and slightly greying, he was the epitome of the English gentleman abroad. His advice was simply, 'Don't go'. We talked the situation out some more and it was generally considered that in a few months time, around June, the situation in the valley would have improved. June is the start of the tourist season, and the only chance for the people to earn enough money to eat throughout the coming winter. We would just have to hedge our bets and wait and see. Adrian's was good advice and we walked away with a telephone number to ring in case we ran into problems.

It was two rather nervous Himalayan runners, therefore, who boarded the plane for Nepal.

As we circled Kathmandu airport before touchdown, I got my first view of the Himalayas. We were going to run through that? In my excitement I forgot about Kashmir, it was a long, long way away and we would deal with it when the time came. For now, we were about to land in the most mountainous country on Earth, and our real preparation could begin.

Kathmandu is like nowhere else in the world. The city just smacks you in the face as soon as you enter. Tiny, windy streets, rickshaws, bicycles, cows, noise, smells and people. Most of all, the people. They are everywhere, all shapes and sizes and colours. It's absolutely fascinating. Most are very poor but manage to eke out a living from buying and selling things. For sale are carpets, clothing, shawls, fruit, shoes, pots and pans, books, pens, etc, etc, etc. It all seems to tumble out onto the street and everything is moving. People are poking around in every nook and cranny. Selling trinkets, washing clothes, washing children, mending things, sewing things, carrying things. The place is a *melee* of human activity. And the activity doesn't stop, it goes on right through the night. Wedding processions, brass bands playing endless pieces of tuneless music, people eating or just moving from A to B, the city never sits still. What a place!

Then we went running.

It's hot and the sweat flies from us as we dash through the tiny streets. We pass staring, slightly amused faces. The watchers are friendly and shout out encouraging words like, 'Hello' and 'You are running!'

There are lots of scraggy-looking dogs, but most are small and don't seem to take any notice of us, which is a blessing. I wonder if they eat dog meat here? Kathmandu life rushes by, and then we are running up the near-vertical steps to the Monkey Temple, legs and arms pumping hard, to emerge at the top doubled-over, sucking in the air. We stand for a couple of minutes gazing out over the rooftops of Kathmandu, then plunge back down, whooping and shouting with glee as we take the steps two or three at a time and run back into the city the long way round.

Another week saw us with a permit to run through Nepal (again the photograph in the *Telegraph* clinched the deal), and the last of the kit drop-offs was organised. We ran and read and cut and sewed. Our kit had to be right before we started. Everything we did not need was cut off. Rucksack straps, labels, pen housings, the lot. Nothing got by untouched. We allowed ourselves just two luxuries. One, a small Union Jack planted proudly on the lid of each pack, and the other, a photo of wife and family. The packs were now down to just eleven pounds each.

Our final training took us high into the hills north of Kathmandu, in amongst the Langtang range. Here we ran and climbed and tested our bodies and our kit for two glorious weeks. My diary exclaims . . .

We are climbing up towards Gosainkund from Sing Gompa. The snow is cold and crisp under our feet and a hot sun blazes from a blue sky. Up around 13,000 feet the air is thin but we have long since acclimatised and are revelling in a new level of fitness. We have reached our target for the day, a tiny prayer flag by a disused wooden hut high up on a windy ridge. All around are white-topped mountains and bottomless valleys and from here I can see right into Tibet.
Tomorrow, we head south, then east to Darjeeling. Our training is now over, it is time at last for our real test to begin.

Chapter 4

SLOW AND STEADY WINS THE RACE

Darjeeling, Queen of the Himalayas. Ancient town, perched on a ridge overlooking the high snowy wastes of Kanjenjunga and the starting point of our journey.

Once we had got off the bus and stretched out our cramped muscles after the twenty-four-hour bone-shaking ride from Kathmandu, Justin exclaimed, 'That's the last bus ride I take for a long time.'

He meant it too, in more ways than one, for we didn't expect to be travelling on anything other than our own two feet for the next hundred days. What a frightening thought!

We had been together now for almost a month, living cheek-by-jowl, and both of us had relaxed. We had been working at our relationship and had learned to accept each other's different ways. We could laugh more easily together and talk about things without the conversation degenerating into an argument. Put simply, we had become more used to each other. Now, with the start only a couple of days away, we were like two excited schoolboys setting out on a big adventure. Both of us had already lost weight and our two weeks up at altitude in Nepal had given us the lean and hungry look of the long distance runner.

Everything had come together at last. We had the permission we needed, extra kit was stashed at three points along the route, and our packs felt featherweight on our backs. We were feeling thoroughly pleased with ourselves and strolled around town with silly grins on our faces.

On 9 March I was twenty-six years old. A mere youth but not able really to use the excuses of youth any more. I opened Leah's letter, which she had given me at the airport, and thought of home.

Darjeeling is steeped in history. Famous for its tea plantations and its Englishness. The British had acquired the district in 1835 from the Raja of Sikkim for an annual fee of 3,000 rupees. The revenue from the land at this time was only 200 rupees, so the Raja got a pretty good deal. But with good management, the tea plantations started to pay good dividends and Darjeeling flourished. The 'Planters' and the 'Gymkhana' Club were established. Here, the mostly British members could find a little piece of England in the middle of the Himalayas.

Justin and I entered the dark and dusty hall of the Gymkhana Club and became members for a day. The place smelled of decay and our voices echoed around the long-disused and empty rooms, but it had retained the mustiness and character of the proverbial Gentlemen's Club. Through the gloom we saw carved wooden panels on the walls, deep armchairs and dusty pictures of old Englishmen with full beards and staring eyes. There is a card room, the green felted tables set out ready for a game, and a large carriage clock hangs on the wall, its pendulum long since at a standstill. It seemed that in this place, time had indeed stopped an age ago.

We played snooker in the dark (Darjeeling has a major problem with its electricty supply), and I lost.

When the British left in 1948, Darjeeling, due to its remote location, had not experienced any industrial growth and the tea plantations soon went into decline. The new owners took their profits to the plains and by 1970 there were few plantations left.

We also visited the Himalayan Mountaineering Institute, a fascinating museum on the history of climbing in the Himalayas. The names lining the walls give testament to the great climbers of the world. I wonder what some of them would have thought of our little venture. We signed the visitors' book as proof of our arrival . . . 'Edward Ley-Wilson and Justin Matterson — Great Britain. From this point we head out west in an attempt to run the entire length of the Himalayas in less than one hundred days. Next stop, Gulmarg. We will do our best.'

Having paid our respects to the grave of the great Tenzing Norgay, who with Sir Edmund Hillary was the first man to reach the top of Mount Everest, we took some photos of each other, posing self-consciously by the main entrance, then jogged back to the hotel.

Tomorrow, 13 March 1990, we would go.

That night I lay awake, my mind churning on what was ahead. I felt excited, satisfied and apprehensive all at the same time. I thought of all the people back home who were rooting for us. Of Leah and my family, of many good friends who were helping to raise money for the charity on our behalf, and of our new-found friends at Intermediate Technology. I was doing this not just for myself, not now, but for all these people who had put their faith in us, I was doing it for them. The sense of responsibility weighed heavy and I felt determined not to let them down. Whatever happened, I would complete.

D-Day. Renamed as DD-Day. Desperate Dash day. This is it at last. Two years of planning, two years of hopes, triumphs, disappointments, frustration and elation and here we are on the start line.

The hotel waiter brought in our breakfast at six o'clock this morning and filled us up with eggs and bread and gallons of tea. He looked with a puzzled expression at our running gear, tiny rucksacks and excited faces.

'Where do you going to so early?' he asked in broken English.

'Gulmarg,' we told him, and fell about laughing.

'You come back in evening?'

This was too much and I fell off the bed.

As we left, the manager of the hotel, who boasted that once upon a time as a waiter he had served potatoes to Princess Anne, warmly shook our hands and wished us good luck. We stepped out into the cold early-morning mist and started to run.

The dirty streets of Darjeeling were suddenly behind us and at last we were alone. Running along the side of the hill and steadily down, the mist turned the world white and wet and eerie. As we appeared out of the gloom, a small group of baboons panicked and scattered into the surrounding forest. Our packs felt featherweight and we ran on a 'high' in anticipation of what was to come.

About ten miles out of town, we came across a sign by the road that said, 'Slow and steady wins the race'. It was an apt saying indeed and we took a photograph with the self-timer, of us beside it, giggling like schoolboys.

Through the bustling transport town of Kurseng and down out of the mist. We are heading for the plains at the foot of the Himalayas, in order to cross into Nepal. Today we will descend over 7,000 feet, all of which will have to be clawed back in the next couple of days.

I feel great and lengthen my stride a little, enjoying the feel of being on the move at last. Justin is more reserved. He is terribly worried about getting injured and has already made it quite clear that if he gets a bad injury, then he will have no compunction in stopping altogether. He is unsure as to whether or not he is capable of doing this run at all. That's the difference between the two of us. I am full of 'go' and self-confidence and probably a deal of over-confidence too, while Justin is reserved and unsure of himself. His comments on stopping altogether fill me with dread, for to do this alone would be incredibly hard and lonely. My commitment to the run is also that much greater as, for the last two years, I have sunk everything into it. Justin has joined me at a relatively late stage and obviously does not yet feel committed. I hope that as we start to leave the miles behind us, he will see just what is being achieved and we can go on together. Right now, I must set the pace and keep us moving forward.

We made thirty miles that first day and stopped at a tiny wooden village called Panighatta down on the plains. 'It is very rare,' say the villagers, 'that any foreigners are seen here.' We sit in the local doctor's house, cross-legged on a mat on the floor, totally immersed in the Indian way of life. The doctor, a bright-eyed, grey-haired man of sixty-two, pushes rice and *daal* (lentils) at us until we are full to bursting. Outside, the banana and mango trees are filled with chirping crickets and the tea plantations stretch away to the horizon.

Today, we have traversed our first mountain, Kanjenjunga, but our elation at the start has vanished.

Chapter 5

THE HIMALAYAN SHUFFLE

From first light we run for hours across the flat plains, through tea plantations, over nearly-dry river beds and past forests choked with scrub and bushes. Brilliant white egrets flap lazily over the ground, parrots in jungle-green screech in the trees and the fluorescent blues and pinks of a jaybird flash in the morning sun. Distant tiny figures bathe in the last remaining pools in the river beds, and a lone cyclist, thin and bolt-upright in the saddle, cycles up, staring with wonder at the two sweating Englishmen running towards him. As he passes he turns right round in the saddle, still staring, and almost disappears off the side of the track.

By midday the heat is sitting on us like a physical weight. It forces the liquid from our bodies and burns on the backs of our necks and arms. We adopt a new phrase for our kind of running, 'The Himalayan Shuffle'.

The 'Shuffle' is a form of running designed to cover maximum distance with minimum effort. The idea is to adapt the running style so that the feet only just leave the ground. There is no real back kick to speak of, and a side view shows someone almost gliding rather than bouncing along. Our 'Himalayan Shuffle' is just over twice as fast as our Himalayan walk, and it works.

We shuffle on to the Nepalese border, losing weight with every step. Karkhabitta – border town. Smelly, noisy and busy, busy, busy. Customs officials on both the Indian and Nepalese sides. I still get that awful sick feeling in the pit of my stomach when dealing with these guys. It stems from my experiences in China. But this

Justin picks his way through a Nepali traffic jam

border post is no real problem for us. It is the one at the other end that is the dodgy one.

Nepal is a different world. From the border post we run west then cut north up towards the village of Brudhabari at the foot of the Himalayas. Baking heat and shuffling feet, and the tea bushes that cloaked the landscape in India are suddenly replaced by paddy fields as we cross the border. The sun glints off the flat wetness all around and we don our sunglasses to keep the glare out of our eyes. A small herd of water buffalo laze in muddy pools and a cheeky white egret balances on one foot on the rump of one. The buffalo doesn't mind the bird as it picks out the irritating ticks from its skin. It's a partnership. The egret gets an easy feed and the buffalo gets a bit of a clean-up. We pass men and women standing shin deep in the muddy fields, pushing the young shoots of rice into the soil. These people are very poor and their rough clothes hang off skeletal frames as they stand up from their work to watch us running by.

We stop at a wooden tea shack at the turning to the north. Black salted tea and potato *momos* are the order of the day. Tea comes in small dirty glasses and I use my finger to wipe some of the boiling liquid over the side of the glass to try and clean it. This becomes a habit with me to such an extent that even back home I still go to stick my finger in my tea before drinking. The glasses were always so dirty that I thought the hot liquid would kill any bugs on the outside before I put it to my lips. Justin thought my curious behaviour was a bit over-the-top.

Both of us were keen not to get ill and we employed the old adage of 'prevention is better than cure'. If we drank the water as it was, we would very quickly get diarrhoea with all the inherent problems of dehydration and sore bottom that that entails. So we decided to carry chlorine tablets and purify all water before drinking. Towards the end of the trip we relaxed a little and drank from snow melt streams, but right now, with approximately 1,950 miles to go, both of us were keen to avoid this unpleasantness if possible. Chlorinated water tastes like swimming pool water but, after ten minutes, it is at least safe.

But by the time we reach Brudhabari, we both have diarrhoea anyway. We've made twenty-seven miles today, have crossed the border and tomorrow will be back into the Himalayas. The village here at the foot of the hills is about six miles off the road but it seems to want for very little. There is a dry, dusty main street, the only traffic being of the four-legged kind, a standpipe and rows of tiny stores selling everything from salt to sandals.

We are now ensconced in a small lodge and a mass of people have come to see the two curiosities. Bronzed, round Nepali faces peer in through the door and an excited babble fills the air. No-one speaks English here, so we communicate with sign-language, using sleeping signs and eating signs to get them to understand what we need. With the help of our few scribbled notes of Nepalese we manage to secure somewhere to sleep the night and, more important at this time, the location of the toilet.

We have decided to have our trousers chopped down to long shorts, and Justin disappears off to find a tailor. That's one of the wonderful things about Nepal: you can get anything done here. Everything is used until it falls apart, then it is mended, re-used, re-mended and so on. They throw nothing away. He found what he was looking for, an old man bent over a sewing machine. Within a few minutes, the trousers had become shorts.

The first few days (note the long shorts)

We decided to wear long shorts for a number of reasons. First, to show too much leg in Nepal is not really the done thing and can offend; second, shorts are much easier to run in than trousers; and third, you can always make long shorts into short shorts.

Justin appeared back at the lodge modelling a fine pair of long, black shorts and a big grin. 'I've just lost us each another pound in weight. How do I look?'

'With those shorts? About ten years old.'

'Older than you then,' came the smiling retort. 'Do you think we'll go any faster now?'

'With this streamlining? Like the wind.'

'I think I'll sell the design to *The Clothes Show* after this trip and retire to somewhere flat.'

We pranced around for a while, checking that the new design didn't rub in any awkward places, then laid out the sleeping bags on our hard wooden beds and slept.

'Up with the sparrow's fart' at half past five to find that the proprietor of the lodge had cooked us up a huge plate of fried noodles each. Great running food, full of carbohydrate.

Last night the bed bugs found me at last. They came at me out of the sun and I didn't stand a chance. I fought back and managed to down a few of them but was soon overwhelmed by numbers as the persistent little pests dug their tiny teeth in all over my body. There was only one thing for it. I leapt up and staggered, scratching and itching, down the rickety ladder that was the staircase and pulled up a bucket of water from the well in the courtyard. This'll fix you, you little beggars, I thought, and poured the water over my head. Instant relief.

We warm up, don the packs and run on. The track soon gives way to a path, then just a scrape in the soil. We have no map of this area bar our 1:1,000,000, which is far too large a scale to be anything more than a general guide. Using the compass we stay on a course roughly north, but the ground is getting steeper and more wooded and the route-finding becomes difficult.

Suddenly, just as we are beginning to despair, the village of Khujunabari looms into view. It is a place straight out of a spaghetti western. A single dirt street lined with a ragtaggle of wooden and mud huts. Chickens peck around in the dust and tiny barefoot kiddies, when they see us coming, run screaming into their mothers' arms. Wizened old men sit in smoke-blackened porches and suck on pipes. Their heads stay still, but their eyes follow us with quiet interest as we move past. There is a small crowd of men gathered around some sacks and a large set of simple balance scales. Their loud bantering stops short as they spot us. We stroll up, with big grins on our faces and greet them in the Nepali way. Hands together and saying 'Namaste'. Their anxious faces break into smiles and we are made welcome.

Sitting on one of the porches, sipping black tea, and surrounded by curious onlookers, a young man pushes his way through and sits down beside me. His name, he tells me, is Rajendra, he is eighteen years old, and is learning English at his college somewhere to the south of here. This is his village and we are welcome. How much is my watch?

Rajendra was a great help. We left his village with a little sketch map of the route to Ilam, our target for the day. His parents had managed to make enough money to send him to school and he was clever enough to continue into further education. But times were difficult now, for his parents needed his help in the fields and he would have to leave his studies for a while until there was enough money in the family coffers for him to return. I wondered how many other young people in Nepal were in a similar predicament. For here was a young man, born into a poor family in a remote village, who, having gone to school, was keen to improve his lot. His education had given him new horizons. Yet at the time when a western boy of the same age would be branching out on his own, Rajendra was drawn by necessity back into the family fold to become what he called 'a simple farmer' again. He was obviously frustrated, but nonetheless philosophical about his fate. 'If I work hard in the fields and we get a good crop, then maybe I can go back to finish my studies.'

'How long will that be?'

'Three, maybe four years. I don't know.'

As we left this simple village with its welcoming people, I felt terribly lucky to be doing what I was doing. Rajendra would never get to go abroad or go on holiday. He was caught in the circle of poverty that affects so much of the world. Yet, purely because of where I was born, I was free to do what I wanted. It could so easily have been me living here in the village instead and I resolved to remember Rajendra if ever I thought that times were tough.

Clutching our new directions, we set off again and start to climb steadily. We run into hilly jungle but the track is clear and we make good progress. The air is filled with a silence that is impossible to experience in England, and the scent of flowers and shrubs is sweet. The jungle floor is a dry, twisted mass of trees, vines, bushes and fallen leaves. Butterflies of all colours flutter about us as we stop to cool ourselves in a trickling jungle stream. The water cools but the sun beats mercilessly down. God, it's hot. It must be in the eighties at least.

Sweat pours out of every pore in our bodies and stains our clothing and rucksacks. I look across at Justin sitting perched on a fallen log on the other side of the tiny stream. He is filthy. We both are. His legs are covered with the dusty earth and his shoes have turned from blue to brown with dirt. He is showing signs of the day's effort. We've already come ten miles today, and his face looks gaunt with the loss of so much liquid. We haven't shaved since the start and the greyness of a coming beard adds to the dishevelled effect. His once-white t-shirt has turned a wet, dirty grey and, where his rucksack straps have sat on his shoulders, there are two white stripes that the dust couldn't reach. Even the rucksack, now lying by his feet, has nasty white sweat marks down each side. 'You need a wash,' I say.

'Likewise.'

We glance at each other and grin.

'It's fun though, isn't it, all this empty space, in the jungle, the wildlife? I hardly have a care in the world out here.' I lie back on the bed of brush and fallen leaves, feel the ants immediately starting to scramble over my arms and under my t-shirt and sit bolt upright again, slapping the hardy little devils off.

'Except for getting eaten alive,' laughs my partner, watching my antics with some amusement.

The water bottle we had filled and chlorinated was now ready and we drank thirstily. There was only a quarter of a litre each, for we had just one half-litre bottle between us. We needed really to drink much more. I had peed only once today and it was a rather dark yellow colour. It should have been white. Yellow means dehydration and that leads to exhaustion and possible heat-stroke, which I have had before a few years ago and it's not much fun. Neither of us liked to stop too often as stopping broke our rhythm, so we tended to splash through most streams and keep going. This was foolish, for we got very tired very quickly and then had to spend time gulping down large quantities of swimming pool water later on. If only it didn't taste so horrible.

We run on. The climbing has begun in earnest now and our legs and lungs groan at us as we push on. The track up the steep slope is rocky and covered with leaves. The leaves hide loose stones and it is an exhausting job to keep going. A Nepali lad of about sixteen appears and starts to run beside us. In fact he runs beside, in front, between and behind us, which is extremely annoying. But he does

Ed route checking

show us the route so I swallow my fury as he cuts in front of me for the fifth time, and keep going. The lad has come from the last village we were in and is heading for Soktim, a remote tea estate only a few miles away now. We are heading that way too and are thoroughly relieved when he loses interest or energy or both and stops for a rest. Within minutes we are too far ahead for him to catch us. Climbing up and up through dappled shadows made by tall fir trees we emerge at last, pouring sweat, at the rather ragged looking tea estate.

A young student, speaking good English and studying technical design at the college in Ilam, sells us dry glucose biscuits and we down more of the swimming pool water. On and up to Chisapani, a tiny, colourful little mud-built village, the orange-coloured houses topped with a shaggy hair of thatch. Dodging and weaving through the chickens and goats; past two scraggy mongrels which put on a show of strength, saliva dripping from hungry bared fangs as they growl and bark from the safety of their bed of roof thatch. On and on we fly, topping the slope to race along a narrow ridge. We are well and truly back in the Himalayas now, with great views of rolling mountains, distant valleys and terraced hill sides.

Then we are descending. Racing down, leaping small boulders and tree roots, sliding on loose rock, down, down to the Mai River. Over the swing bridge we cut down the bank, strip off and plunge into the cold, clear blue torrent. What bliss! In the forest around us, birds of fluorescent blues and reds and yellows do acrobatics in the sky above our heads, dragonflies whirr on invisible wings and high up, a bearded vulture soars on spiralling thermals.

Refreshed and reinvigorated, we set off up the final hill of the day. The sun begins to dip behind the surrounding hills and our sweat turns cold and clammy on our chests. Only a few minutes up from the river, tired legs begin to reassert themselves and near-empty stomachs grumble for food. Justin is feeling it. His feet are sore, he is still thirsty as hell, he feels giddy and light-headed, and he has no compunction in having a good moan about it all. I try to keep things cheery and jolly him along, but this is no picnic and he's going to have to accept that or he's going to have a miserable few months. We plod upwards and by the time we get to the hilltop village of Ilam I'm having severe misgivings about spending another ninety-seven days with my partner.

My problem is that I'm too impatient with people, indeed most of the time I'm pretty impatient with myself. The last three years in industry, managing different types of people, have given me an ability to control these feelings and I try to regard each person as an individual. Everyone has good and bad points, including me. It's just that at this stage of the expedition I was having trouble in spotting any of my partner's good points. He would go on and on about how he just wanted to go slowly so as to minimise the risk of injury. I pointed out to him that I didn't mind going slowly as long as we reached the day's target. The trick is not to go so slowly that we have to keep going into the night.

'Look, Justin,' I was boiling with anger inside for I'd had this moaning all the way up the hill, 'I don't mind going slowly at all, but we have to reach each day's target. If we don't then we won't make the hundred days. It's as simple as that. Anyway it's likely we are both going to feel rotten many times during this trip so we may as well get used to it.'

Justin, to his credit, for he was obviously feeling pretty awful, was most positive about it. 'Oh, I'll keep going all right, but your legs are more used to this type of running than mine, that's all.'

It was true. I had my Chinese experience to draw on and my legs were conditioned to this type of rough treatment. Justin's were not, not yet anyway, and I needed to remember that. Little did I know at this stage that later on in the trip, it would be me doing the suffering and Justin setting the pace. But right now I felt the need to keep pushing on. If we set a poor pace at the start of the run, then as we got more and more tired we were likely to get slower. I felt that it was crucial for us to put in some long days at the start, to get our bodies used to the punishment. If we lost time now, then it would be almost impossible to make it up again later on. We must keep going. I must keep us going. If we could hack this first section to Kathmandu in a good time then we could hack the lot. Back in Britain, we had estimated twenty-three or twenty-four days to Kathmandu, but right now I didn't have a clue if that was feasible. It was only Day Three and already we were feeling the strain.

Ilam was a haven for tired limbs and empty bellies. We found a standpipe and some soap and washed socks and feet, then having shovelled huge piles of cold pasta down our gullets, we collapsed into the sleeping bags and slept until dawn.

Day Four passed in a blur of movement and we made thirty-five miles, the last ten of which were all downhill. It's an amazing feeling running downhill for ten miles. You just can't do that in Britain. As we climbed through the morning and into the afternoon

I consoled myself with the old adage, 'What goes up must come down' and my wish came true. After the knee-bending, bone-shaking, thigh-aching descent to Phidim, we collapsed flat out on the floor of a local inn, scarcely breathing, eyes closed, relishing the sensation of having the weight off our feet.

We put our feet up on our rucksacks so that the blood and liquid that had dripped down during the day, can flow back out of the legs again. The feeling of relief is almost indescribable, and we lie there watching our knees and ankles twitch involuntarily with the effort they have put in. My body is tingling, crying out for grub (so what's new?), and my knees hurt.

We woke to Day Five and our bodies told us that it was to be a hard day. Crawling stiffly out of our sleeping bags at half past five, we stood up on wavering limbs, secretly wondering what on earth we were doing out here trying to run the Himalayas. It was only Day Five and, although we had achieved good mileage so far, I wondered if my body could really handle this sort of punishment for the next ninety-five days. Why hadn't I said that we would run from Darjeeling to Kathmandu, then see, instead of telling everyone that we'd run all the way? Another 350-odd miles was a tangible target. I could visualise the distance in my mind's eye, but another 1,900, that was too much. I shook myself out of this self-imposed depression and found I had automatically started to do the stretching exercises that had become a morning ritual.

'How are the limbs, matey?' I asked Justin.

'Ask me again in a few minutes,' came the sleepy reply.

He was standing on one foot, the other placed on a ledge at waist height, trying desperately to push his head down onto the raised knee. We were silent for a few minutes, the silence broken by a single cock crow and by the small puffing and gasping sounds that came from our lips as we knotted ourselves into strange shapes. Two tiny Nepali children appeared at the doorway. Their eyes were still heavy with sleep but when they saw us, the sleep fell away and they stared open-mouthed at the two strange Englishmen tying themselves into knots. Gradually the stiffness disappeared from our muscles and within half an hour we were ready to go.

Munching on a small packet of glucose biscuits, we headed out of the village and into east Nepal. We were passing through a land of enormous ridges and deep valleys. To a normal trekker this part of Nepal may seem rather empty, but to us it was a maze of paddy

fields and small homesteads, and when we saw paddy fields we
knew that people had to be nearby. Here the Kiranti people make a
living from working the land. They grow rice, corn, millet, barley,
wheat and potatoes and everything is done by hand. The fields are
carved from the hillsides to form flat terraces, which climb 2,000
feet up the sides of the spurs like some giant's stairway. The work of
tilling, planting and picking is hard and the reward is a living, for
these people eat almost everything they grow. Any surplus is sold
in order to buy other essentials such as material for clothes, or
perhaps a goat or chickens. It is a life of bare subsistence, a life that
we in the West have long since forgotten.

When we ran into an area where the fields were being farmed,
the track could disappear suddenly and without trace. We were
faced with trudging ankle deep through the soggy, muddy paddy
fields or back-tracking. The back-tracking route was usually
adopted.

Today is a day full of paddies. We run through a glorious green
garden of fields. The sun glints off the water and the green of the
rice-shoots lights up the greyish brown soil. Dotted in amongst the
green are homesteads, mud-built homes stained a rich russet and
white, dusty courtyards, chickens, the odd cow and goats galore,
ladies weaving or threshing or stripping corn from the cob, and
young girls balancing metal water jugs on their hips and their
heads. As we run by we smile and wave and they smile back. The
tiny children's cries of 'Namaste', usually yelled at the top of their
voices, carries up and down to us from fields high and low. The
women seem to dress much more traditionally than the men. Their
bright skirts and heavy coats splash yellows and reds over the
landscape, bobbing bits of colour on a far slope as they bend and
straighten while planting the rice.

We stop at one of the homesteads to ask directions in our pathetic
pidgin Nepali. A wrinkled and aggressive old lady immediately
comes at us shouting and waving a small hand-scythe. She
probably doesn't get too many tall, lanky, sweaty westerners
around here and she has daughters to protect. Keeping my eyes on
the scythe I put my hands together as a sign of welcome and give
her my best smile, lots of teeth. This always wins them over, I think.
But the old crone is not to be put off and the scythe is flashed again
in my general direction. She is obviously furious about something.
As she shakes with rage, ranting and raving, her intricately carved

nose rings bounce around and her twisted angry toothless mouth spits venom. The smile freezes on my lips. 'What have I done wrong?' I say sideways to my partner.

'I don't know, but I'd keep watching that scythe if I were you,' says Justin.

We back off slowly, rather bewildered at it all.

'Maybe it's your trousers,' suggests Justin. 'She just doesn't like the pattern.'

'Judging by the look of those daughters of hers, I think it's what's in the trousers that she's worried about.'

'The scythe is about the right size, then.'

At that we turn and disappear at double speed out of the courtyard and out of sight.

Wondering how on earth we were going to get the directions we needed, we start to climb up the hillside, heading towards some men who are planting the fields higher up the slopes.

A sudden loud whistle stops us in our tracks. Back down at the turn in the track, just before the old crone's house, a man is waving at us. 'Maybe they've changed their minds,' says Justin.

We stumble back down onto the track and the man beckons us into the courtyard. This time Justin goes in first. The man has just come from the fields and his arms and legs are covered with black mud, which is fast drying to a light brown colour in the sun. A broad brow and wide nose are outdone by the widest smile I've ever seen, as he bids us sit on a couple of staw mats in the porch.

The old lady is still about, clucking away like an angry hen, but the daughters are nowhere to be seen. Then another man arrives, a young chap of about twenty, with dark skin and sticky-out ears. He speaks a little English and we soon find out the reason for the old lady's animosity towards us. Apparently, the day before, two men had appeared during the night, taken the family's prize goat and made off. This sounded a terribly un-Nepali thing to happen, especially out here in the hills, for the hill people of Nepal are renowned for their honesty and kindness, but happen it did. The old lady had seen two strangers coming through her gate, assumed the worst and attacked, scythe at the ready. It was an unfortunate misunderstanding. The man with the mud was her son. He had heard the commotion from down the hill, where he had been tilling a field by hand, and had rushed up to see what it was all about. He was a simple man, but realised that we were harmless and wanted to make amends.

The salted tea arrives in two small metal cups and we sip contentedly, staring out over the hills. The old crone bends over a mud stove, stoking the fire with precious wood and boiling up more water. Like the stove, the whole house is built of packed mud. The outside of it is painted a bright orange up to the first floor level, then white up to the thatched roof. Doors and windows are lined with a dark wood and shuttered. A porch runs the length of the front of the building and this too is topped with thatch and as I look up I can see the sun glinting through gaps in the straw. All around me are the fruits of these peoples' work. A bundle of wood neatly stacked in a corner and covered with rough-hewn planks to keep off the rain; a basket, woven from bamboo strips, sits upside-down on the ground, trapping a mother hen and her brood; a grinding stone with small residues of powdered grain, evidence of the morning's work; a glinting metal water jug; a rack of drying corn; and a wooden plough leaning up against the side of the house, its metal spike worn from cutting a thousand furrows. Inside the house, shafts of light from the open windows pierce the gloom and light up rows of wooden and metal jugs of different sizes, bundles of clothes and bedding, two short-handled hoes and more of those hand-scythes all sit on a dusty floor. There is no electricity, no glass in the windows and no water tap.

The man with the ears is now squatting by a pile of bamboo stalks. We had seen huge clumps of bamboo around most villages. Some of the stalks had grown to fifty feet in height and were thick as trees at their base. The man starts to split the stalks lengthways by pushing the end of them onto a scythe held between his feet. The thin but strong slats will eventually be fashioned into baskets and mats.

We sit with the mud-covered man, sip tea and discuss, with much gesticulation and misunderstanding, the route for the rest of the day. Armed, once again, with more scribbled directions, the man shows us the way through the paddy fields and then leaves us to go back to his work. We offer him some rupees to pay for the tea but he will not accept. I wonder if we have abused his hospitality by offering money.

The path led us over ridge after ridge, over the grain of the land. We had only water to drink and no food since the glucose biscuits of this morning. This was remote eastern Nepal. Remote it is but uninhabited it is not and we began to feel at home in amongst it all.

Topping yet another ridge, we stopped where a tiny stream of

Steamy green slopes in eastern Nepal

water trickled over a rock. Someone had jammed a stick of bamboo under the rock and some of the water dribbled off the end of this. We stuck our heads underneath and cooled off.

I stood up and shivered with delight as the cold water ran down my back. Wiping the water from my eyes I blinked and looked up. A filing cabinet was coming up the hill towards me. I blinked again. Yes, it was a filing cabinet, bobbing up and down as it climbed the hill. 'There's a filing cabinet coming up the hill, Justin.'

'You've had too much sun, Ed, have a sit down.'

'No, seriously, come and see.' As we watched, the cabinet turned a corner in the steep track and underneath it was a little man with thin, wiry legs staggering under the weight. He was hot and we could see the beads of sweat covering his arms and face. Five minutes later he had reached the little stream, carefully sat the cabinet on a ledge of rock and wriggled out from under his head harness to have a rest and a drink. We thought we had it pretty tough but this guy brought us right back down to size. He grinned at us and brought two spindly arms together in the traditional Nepali greeting, then sat and had a smoke.

In Nepal, everything has to be carried in by hand. Only a tiny portion of the country has any kind of road system, for the nature of the terrain is such that road building is almost impossible in most areas. So if you live in a remote village and you want a new filing cabinet or a corrugated iron roof or whatever, then it all has to be carried in on the backs of animals or men. The Nepalese get used to carrying things from a very young age so by the time they are adults they are capable of lifting incredibly heavy loads. Later on in the trip we were to meet people who carried loads of as much as 200lbs.

Nepali children are prepared for a life of carrying at a very young age

The weight is taken by a strap placed around the forehead so all the strain goes on the back of the neck. It is a traditional way of carrying things, practised by different peoples all over the world.

The wiry man with the filing cabinet had finished his cigarette and was carefully fitting himself back into his harness. Taking the strain he lifted the cabinet free of the ground, wavered slightly, then plodded slowly off down the track.

We shouldered our tiny, eleven-pound packs, which now looked pretty pathetic, and set off the other way.

Three hours later we had descended to the Tamur River and in another one-and-a-half hours we staggered in the quickly gathering darkness into the village of Dobhan. It had been a hard day.

If yesterday had been hard work then today was simply exhausting: a seven-hour climb with no food and just enough water to keep us going. Our mouths dried out and it became hard to swallow. We climbed up through fields of rice, past smaller and smaller homesteads. In one shady glade, where water trickled off the end of a bamboo spout, a young woman was washing herself, breasts hanging heavily and long black hair covered with soap suds. She did not hear or see us coming and we passed by on the narrow track, being as discreet and quiet as possible so as not to alarm her.

The Nepali people are extremely shy when it comes to bodily functions. Washing is never done completely naked. Just one part of the body is bared at a time and the genitals are washed under a skirt or, in the men's case, under a loose robe. It is considered offensive for anyone to bare their private parts. Before we left Britain I had read about a young French couple who had gone trekking in the Himalayas. Finding the weather hot enough, the lady stripped down to a teeny-weeny bikini and the man to a small black thong. They then re-donned their walking boots and continued. Needless to say, the young couple attracted much attention but were unable to get anywhere to sleep for the night. The Nepali people just didn't want to know.

For us, though, washing was an important part of the day. We were washing bodies and clothes at every opportunity, for to keep clean maintains high morale and helps prevent illness and infection.

We washed the Nepali way. First, find your water supply. Second, check upstream to ensure there's no outside toilet discharging its effluent into the water. Third, start to wash. We would take off one article of clothing at a time, soak it, soap it and soak it again. Then we would scrub our filthy sweaty bodies before donning the now clean but wet item of clothing and allowing our body heat to dry it off. It was a rather cold way to keep clean, but it worked. We couldn't wash down below in public, so that part of us had to wait until we found a suitably remote stream the next day. Both of us had diarrhoea on a regular basis now, indeed it had

Justin staggers under a 200lb load of pots and pans

become a part of everyday life and provided an extra spur to keep clean.

We have climbed high above any fields and homesteads, on and up into the sky. The vegetation is changing as we go higher. Down in the valleys there were banana trees and bamboo, but up here, the trees are smaller and twisted, rhododendrons cloak the slopes in red and mosses colour the trees different shades of green and brown. We have seen no-one for hours now and it's worrying to think that we might be on the wrong track. We stop at every vantage point and stare up at the hill, searching for the top. The map shows a track heading in a north-westerly direction up to the pass. The track we are on twists and turns to such an extent that it is difficult to say what is our general direction. We will have to wait and see. Both of us are very tired now and our bodies feel like dead things as we trudge upwards, long since slowed to a painful walk by the aggressive gradient.

One of our ten-minute rest-stops found us both laid flat out on the track, arms and legs splayed wide.

'I think I'll stay here the night,' joked Justin. 'It's Sunday tomorrow: does that mean we get a lie in?' He raised his head and looked at me with a grin.

'It's Sunday today.'

He lowered his head back down. 'Oh!'

'I could die here and die happy.' I was so very tired and the feeling of being still was wonderful. My stomach grumbled away and my mouth felt sticky with dried saliva.

'I wonder what everyone's up to at home now,' said Justin.

'Roast chicken, potatoes, peas and sweetcorn, that's what my lot are up to,' I said.

'Followed by blackberry and apple pie.'

'Then more roast chicken.'

'Another slice of pie, and cheese and biscuits, and coffee to round it all off.'

'Oh no, this is too much,' I exclaimed. We were both laughing weakly, staring up at the sky and visualising the feast.

'I'm not actually that hungry,' I said nonchalantly, my stomach craving food.

'Liar.'

We lay there and laughed and bantered away like two old friends. The usual awkwardness between us disappeared at times like this and it was good to be there together.

I rolled onto my stomach and pushed myself weakly up onto hands and knees. Why was everything such an effort? Feet on the ground, I hauled myself upright. A round of applause from my partner, who still lay spreadeagled on the ground. Then he too was up and we trudged onwards together.

At last we came over the top of the pass. This was the Milke Danda, a range of mountains running north and south at a height of 10,000 feet or more. The trees had fallen away beneath us and the Himalayas unfolded all around. We were truly on the roof of the world. The views were endless, we could see a hundred miles, perhaps much more, in any direction. Green ridges gave way to marching blue ones, the whole topped by snow-covered giants. We revelled in the feeling of space and, having spotted the summer village of Gupha away on the other side of the bowl that was the pass, began to run again.

The promise of food put a spring in our step and before long we sat in a tiny wooden hut hungrily tucking into huge piles of rice and *daal*. I began to perk up. With every mouthful I could feel the energy building back up inside me. 1,500 grammes of rice each later, we were completely bloated and Justin started to relate Monty Python's *Mr Creosote* sketch. This is a scene in which a fat man walks into a posh restaurant, orders the entire menu and proceeds to shovel it down by the plateful. As the meal progresses he grows larger and larger and eventually, after forcing down a 'wafer-thin after-dinner mint', bursts. A strange tale indeed.

The people up here on the pass look different from those in the valleys we have just left. They are Tibetan and obviously Buddhist, for prayer flags abound. We think they may be Lhomi people of the BhoTiya, the true Himalayan Highlanders. Their ancestors would have come from Tibet around the fourteenth century to inhabit the high valleys and passes. They practised high-altitude farming and yak and sheep husbandry, practices which are still continued today. It is only a small community up here on the pass and I presume that they must have other homes lower down the slopes for in the winter this pass would be covered with snow and must be a thoroughly inhospitable place.

Gupha is a staging post for those engaging in long-distance trade. There are a number of tea shacks and the people buzz around looking very busy. The Tibetan people in Nepal are renowned for being business-minded and, judging by the number of shacks, there must be some business to be had up here.

We run headlong down the other side of the pass, suddenly full of energy. Within minutes the Tibetan prayer flags, yaks with tinkling bells and high pastures were far behind us. Down, down, down, flying over the rocky track. I lead and set a strong pace, pushing it on, Justin is right on my heels all the way. He has been getting fitter and stronger by the day and it seems that his ankles and knees have strengthened to the extent that he can now skim over the rough terrain. We are slowly evening out.

Eventually we come down to the village school at Nundhaki, a small open square of dusty mud buildings perched on the only available flat piece of ground. The kids come rushing out to greet us and we are suddenly surrounded by a babble of high-pitched, chattering voices. The teacher appears from a doorway in one of the buildings and directs us further down the hill to where we can find somewhere to sleep for the night.

The track is only just off the vertical and we stumble down into the tiny cluster of houses that is Nundhaki. Having asked an old man, a young boy, a lady and a water buffalo where to stay the night, we eventually find sanctuary in a splendid mud- and wood-built house, presided over by a neatly dressed man of about fifty. In the past the man had been a member of that most respected and feared force, the Gurkhas. Today as in years past this British regiment still recruits hundreds of young Nepali men to fight for the Crown. Feared for their skill and decisiveness in battle, the Gurkhas have won their laurels in many parts of the world and the hills of Nepal are full of these men who have served their time in another country's army. The man welcomes us in and gives us a room and plenty of tea. *Daal baat* is being prepared and he brings us *Dongba*, a maize wine, in two small oak caskets. A bamboo straw pokes out of a hole in the lid and we suck away. It is revolting and highly potent.

The sunset paints the clouds orange then pink and bathes the distant hills, over which we must travel tomorrow, in colour. Within an hour we are suspended in the inky blackness of night. On the surrounding hills, tiny flickering lights betray shepherds' cooking fires and the sky lights up with a thousand stars. A cool breeze dries our newly washed clothes and I sit out alone in the porch, listening to the silence. My thoughts turn to home and to my Leah. I wonder what she is doing now, how she is feeling. I know she will be missing me as much as I miss her. I wish she were here now with me, sitting here in the quiet, drinking in the peace of the place. I lay my head back against the mud wall of the house and dream nice dreams.

I am going to see her soon anyway, for she is coming out to do a trek of her own. She has joined an organised trekking company's 'Arun to Everest' trek and flies out to Kathmandu at the beginning of April. We have arranged that Justin and I time our arrival in Kathmandu to meet her. It's all a bit touch-and-go, as our running schedule is based on guesswork, but it will be great if it works. Tomorrow will see us at Tumlingtar, the S.T.O.L. airstrip above the Arun River, where Leah's trek begins.

When all this is over, the two of us will have shared something special. In the past it was always me who went away and Leah who stayed at home minding the fort and raising money for the charity involved. It meant that I had experiences in which she could not possibly share. But this trip should be different. We will both have experienced the Himalayas in our own individual way and although we are apart now, when we come together again, we will have our own impressions of the place to share with each other. I must try to make Kathmandu on time.

'Strange yearnings to travel are dancing lessons from God.'
Stephen Venables

Chapter 6

THE COMMUTER

I stood gasping for air, absolutely knackered, at the end of the five-mile run. The other instructors milled around, obviously having had a fairly easy time of it today. The big man came pounding in to the finish, working hard and puffing like a steam train. He walked past the group of young men, some of whom were hardly sweating, grasped the contents of his shorts and glared at his young instructors. 'When you get into the shower this morning, check you've still got some of these, because I don't think you have.'

This was John Ridgway, yachtsman and explorer extraordinaire. This was his Adventure School and I was the Chief Instructor for 1986. The last twenty-two years of my life had been a search for something new and a series of events had brought me here to the far north-west of Scotland where I had found the space that I needed at last.

Having been brought up in the affluent south-east of England, my childhood home was one of closeted comfiness. My parents had moved regularly from one house to another, but we always lived in the countryside. Holidays were spent out in the surrounding fields with binoculars and a notebook, bird-watching, and dreaming of the Amazon and of African plains. As I grew into my teens the feathered birds were replaced by the smooth, curvy kind and for a while the binoculars were left hanging in a cupboard.

At eighteen, I tried commuting. Well, around where I lived everyone was doing it. I had a job in London, in the City, doing market research for an industrial magazine. Up at six o'clock, on the train by seven to sit in silence in a smoke-filled carriage, pretending to read my *Times*, before making a complete fool of myself as soon as I tried to turn the pages. Five past eight, out into the *melee* of Victoria Station, sweat stains already starting to appear on my neatly pressed shirt collar. Down into the tube to push and shove with a million other sweating, suited City men and women, up the other side, then a mad dash through the car exhausts to arrive dirty, smelly and dishevelled at the office, ready for a day's work. I did this for just four months and vowed to myself that I would never commute again.

About this time I secured myself a place in the Royal Marines. I was to be a Second Lieutenant under training in the batch entitled 'Young Officers May '84'. Suddenly I was thrown into a world of men not boys. Lympstone, the Royal Marines training base, is an active unit and trains both officers and Marines. It was time to grow up.

My colleagues were a mishmash of British society. That's the good thing about the Marines, it doesn't matter a jot whether your father was in the Corps or whether or not you've got a personal income. Here, there were no preconceived ideas and you just survived on your own wits.

For a year I climbed ropes and crawled around in gorse bushes, marched through the night, dug trenches in the rain, studied military tactics and law and history and first aid, rode in helicopters and rigid raiders, laid ambushes, jumped off bridges and got completely drunk on Saturday nights. Sometimes I got it right and sometimes I got it wrong, but I was learning.

I had a number of debilitating injuries just as the final month-long Commando Course started. This course was the make-or-break period for us all. A series of mental and physical tests interspersed with demanding exercises out in the field, and culminating in the award of the Green Beret. Alas for me it was not to be. I was still suffering the disturbing blackouts that had plagued me during the long exercises out in the field, and my current injuries kept me in the military hospital staring out of the window and wondering what it was all about. I left in March 1985.

Looking back, I had been far too young and immature to make a real go of it. Out of fifteen eager young men who had joined in May 1984, only six eventually passed out. It was the only real failure in my life so far. I had dreamed of joining the Royal Marines since the age of sixteen and now that dream was shattered. I had to find something else to do.

A year and a half later I was gasping at the end of the five-mile run up in Scotland, listening to John berate his young instructors for not trying hard enough. I lived in a tiny wooden hut perched on a bank by the sea, which had no electricity or heating. In the winter the ice would form an inch thick on the window panes and when I woke in the morning my eyebrows would be frosted with frozen vapour. The school ran Outward Bound type courses for young people and adults alike and it tested my organisational abilities and my patience to the limit.

For me it was the emptiness, the barrenness that kept me there. I loved the feeling of space and wilderness in the north west Highlands and I found great stimulation and satisfaction in travelling alone over this desolate land. Whenever possible I would don running shoes and rucksack and disappear for the day to run wild and free over the lonely mountains. I got a kick out of getting to the top of a hill, of racing full tilt and barely in control down scree slopes, and of standing on the edge of massive sea cliffs, yelling defiance at the stinging Atlantic winds. One day, in the future, I would find a way to live up here for good.

The season came to an end and it was time now for me to take my life into my own hands. I went south and joined one of the country's best-known food manufacturers, United Biscuits, in Luton.

It was a big change in life-style. Luton, an industrial town thirty miles north of London and at the heart of the consumer society, was like a foreign country to me. I stayed for three years, doing my time, serving my apprenticeship and gaining much experience in the world of industrial training. The firm was good to me and gave me leave to run the Great Wall of China in 1988. In return I gave them long hours and the best work that I could do.

But even after the China trip I needed to do something big. I needed to prove to myself that I was capable of persevering and completing a major undertaking. Maybe my failure in the Royal Marines had spurred me to attempt these gruelling, long-distance challenges. That, coupled with an overpowering need to be out in the open – I don't know. All I do know is that the satisfaction of being able to point to a map of the world and say, 'I did that', is something not to be missed.

When travelling in the remote parts of the world I can feel a freedom that seems to have disappeared in everyday life in Britain. Out here I can be my own boss. If I make a mistake there is no-one to blame but myself, no work place eating away at my soul, no daily scrum on the commuter trains, no advertising or television to clutter my mind. There are the mountains and the sky and wide open spaces where I can find room to breathe and freedom to be whatever I want to be. In the civilised world back home, the pressure to conform is almost overpowering yet it is not for me. I shall choose my own way and although at fifty I may have some aches and pains I will have lived.

Chapter 7

SETTING THE PACE

Day Seven in the Himalayas and I was certainly living a life of my choosing. The ex-Gurkha had given us some rice and omelette in a plastic bag and when we stopped at the first stream for a botty-wash, we also had a great feed. This was only the second time in the trip that we had eaten at the start of the day.

Justin was feeling good today but the food soon put a stop to that. Even food affects the two of us differently. My metabolism eats it up very quickly and gives me the energy I need almost immediately, but Justin's is slower. When he eats, the food sits at the bottom of his stomach for a while before it does anything. That leaves him bloated and burping and thoroughly uncomfortable. Then a couple of hours later he gets the energy return. By this time I have used up much of the energy from the earlier food and am usually ready for more.

We run up and down, over the marching blue hills of the eastern Himalayas. The lower parts of the steep-sided slopes glisten with paddy fields and these give way to thick tree cover as we climb. Rhododendrons splash red on the green and butterflies abound, colouring the air with yellow and blue and brown and white polka-dot. Far below, a river roars foaming over the rocks and as we descend to cross by the rotting swing bridge, a dipper, bright orange tail flashing, darts on stubby wings from rock-pool to rock-pool searching out its lunch.

We are running through the ridgetop village of Chainpur. I am in front, shuffling along on tired legs and Justin is just a couple of metres behind. People stop and stare and smile or, if they are under five years old, they dash madly for their mothers' skirts as soon as they see us coming. We pass hot, panting dogs that take no notice and carry on down to Kharang.

In the village, I was running past a small tea shack when a little black mongrel that seemed to be fast asleep on the porch leapt up and came at me, sinking its teeth into my calf. Angry? I was bloody furious. It was only Justin's intervention that stopped me braining the snarling beast with a rock. The bite had drawn blood and the immediate worry was . . . RABIES. Ranting and raving, foaming at the mouth, raging thirst, pains in the joints, madness then . . . death! Oh well, it was good while it lasted. I was shaking with anger that I'd allowed such a thing to happen. How stupid of me. I should have seen the dog and walked past it instead of running. Justin went off to try and find the offending mutt, which had disappeared in amongst the wooden shacks that lined this part of the route. I sat down on the side of the track and pulled the small medical kit from my rucksack. The bite was stinging and a small trickle of blood had run down my leg and stained my sock. I cleaned the bite up and daubed it with antiseptic. Justin arrived. 'I've seen the dog and it doesn't look rabid to me.'

'What does it look like?'

'Small, round and fluffy really.'

'If I had my way, the damn thing would be small, flat and fluffy by now.'

'What are you going to do? The nearest doc is miles away.'

'Well look, I've had the jab and if the dog doesn't look to be rabid then it should be OK, surely?'

'Yeah, except the jab only prevents the disease taking hold immediately. I think we've got 3 days to get you to a place with a vaccine.'

'That means Kathmandu doesn't it?'

'I'm afraid so.'

'Forget it. I'm not stopping now, not for some little, black, fluffy pooch. The dog's not rabid, I put antiseptic on almost immediately, and if it does get bad, then in three days' time we should be at Lukla anyway. If I had to, I could fly from there.'

'Well, it's your life.'

'Yes it is, isn't it.'

I got up and ran on, keen not to let the injury seize up before the end of the day. It stung but otherwise felt fine. I was confident that it was just a scrape.

Tumlingtar passed underfoot and before long we had crossed the Arun River. For millennia its wide, grey-green waters have flowed out of Tibet, cutting a valley right through the Himalayas to discharge itself eventually into the mighty Ganges on the Indian plain.

We crossed by dugout canoe, our first non-foot transport of the trip so far. The ferryman, this being a service for the local people, dropped us off on a sandy beach and pointed us towards some high banks of jungle brush. This was the short-cut up to Dingla, our target for the day. Needless to say that 'short-cut' means 'hardly used' and 'hardly used' means 'overgrown', and 'overgrown' means 'lost'. Having 'shuffled' up a maze of tiny stream beds, ducked under and climbed over fallen trees, slipped and scrambled up a near-vertical bank, cutting our arms and ripping the t-shirts, we finally ended up on the top of a wooden ledge looking down at another river 1,000 feet below. Except that it wasn't another river. It was the Arun. We had come full circle and had not even realised.

Out came the compass, and we did some logical thinking and some searching for a track, any track. Then we set off, compass in hand, determined to try and get back on course, without having to return to the ferryman to ask for help.

3,000 feet higher and two hours later we staggered into Dingla, terribly tired and badly needing a wash. We had made it, but resolved never to let this happen again. We were both feeling so dead that we tucked ourselves up in our sleeping bags and were asleep by half past seven.

The day dawned cold and wet and my sleep-filled eyes settled on my partner, who sat in the gloom carefully rubbing a badly swollen ankle. He looked very worried and winced with pain as his fingers found a sensitive spot. 'What's up, Justin?' I asked quietly.

He hadn't seen me wake and started, 'Oh it's nothing, just a sore ankle. It'll be OK.'

'Where does it hurt?' I asked.

'Well, it's the Achilles tendon actually. It's not too bad at the moment but I think I'm going to have to take it easy on the downs. That's when I felt it go yesterday.'

I scrambled out of my lovely warm bag into the cold morning. 'Well, you call the shots today. If you want to go slow, just say so.'

'I will, but I think I'm OK, really.'

But he was not OK. After the first hour's running, I could see that he was in some pain. He put a brave face on it and kept going.

Often we stopped at streams and he would take off his shoes and socks and bathe the ankle in cold water. We also made use of the elasticated bandage in our medical kit.

We ran and walked today for nine hours, excluding three hours of stops for food and foot-bathing and drinking. After twenty miles of vicious terrain and difficult route-finding, we climbed 2,000 feet up above the village of Phedi, which means 'bottom of hill' and are now ensconced in a small mud hut along with the Nepali family who live here. They are charming folk living unbelievably hard lives. Mother, a tired-looking but smiling lady dressed in a loose red blouse, heavy waistcoat and a coarse green wool skirt, rules the household entirely. Eldest son and daughter do most of the work, while father lies beside the fire, wrapped in blankets. I think he must be ill for he has hardly moved all evening and looks terribly thin. Mother bustles around in the dark, giving orders for this or that to be done. We spot the other four children in the corner of the hut. Three are toddlers and one is just a baby. Six, then, altogether; two boys and four girls. The two eldest are grinding corn, gathering wood, filling pans with water and spinning wool between their fingers. Mother looks after the others and when the rice is cooked, she ladles out small amounts onto metal plates. The baby needs smaller foods and mother chews up her rice then, placing her own mouth onto her baby's, she feeds the little one her own masticated meal. We are given a simple *daal baat* and shovel it hungrily into our mouths with our fingers. The hut is full of smoke now and everyone's eyes are smarting and watering. My sleeping bag is laid out on some animal skins in one corner of the room and, as I drift off to sleep, the rain is drumming gently on the roof and the family are gathered around the fire, chatting quietly.

The next two days passed in a blur of movement and aching limbs. As we move further west the land gets bigger and more grand. The valleys are deeper and the passes higher. We traverse our second mountain, Makalu, and cross three passes, the Salpa, the Surke and the Chutok La. We run in snow for the first time since our training a lifetime ago, and climb up and down touching 10,000 feet, descending, then up again to 11,000, our bodies acclimatising all the time.

Justin's ankle seems to be holding out, but only just. He bathes it regularly and is very slow coming downhill, but he is still going. The worry of it is getting to him slowly, and he complains about 'these bloody switchbacks' as the path zigzags around the side of enormous spurs. My leg is fine and I have no ill effects from the dog bite.

One particularly nasty section involved travelling from the

village of Guidel to the village of Bung. We stood at Guidel and looked across at Bung on the other side of the valley. It was so close we could almost reach out and touch it. But to get there involved an enormous drop down a near-vertical rocky slope to cross the Hongu Khola (river) before climbing back up the other side. I recalled a quote from H.W. Tilman's book *Nepal Himalaya*.

> *For dreadfulness, naught can excel*
> *The prospect of Bung from Guidel;*
> *And words die away on the tongue*
> *When we look back on Guidel from Bung.*

We have crossed over the watershed from the Arun Valley and are now racing down towards the Everest river, the Dudh Kosi. I am loving every minute of this running. I am as tired and sore as I've ever been but the fresh air, the daily challenge, the massive mountains, rivers and forests put me on a near-permanent high.

Justin, by contrast, is in some pain although he asks for no concessions and is running better than ever. But he feels terribly unsure about what to do. Will the ankle get better or worse? Should he stop and rest? Should he keep going? The insecurity of it all is worrying enough for me, let alone for him. We sit and talk about the possible alternatives but whatever I may think, the decision has got to rest with him. Only he knows the pain involved so only he can decide whether he should stop or continue. I try to be as supportive as possible but there's little I can do to help. I find it hard to control my natural impatience and I have to keep holding myself back. We are still on target, for today is Day Ten and in a few hours we will have reached Lukla on the run-in to Everest.

Ten days right across eastern Nepal, over the grain of the most mountainous country on earth. Ahead of us lies a dangerous dash up to Kala Pattar, the hill overlooking Everest Base Camp, then a supreme effort over three major passes to reach Kathmandu in time to see Leah and get some news from home.

Pounding down to the tiny community of Kharte, we were like downhill slalom skiers, taking blind turns at full speed and changing direction at every twist in the dusty track.

Coming up towards us were two rather clean-looking light blue t-shirts. Dick Smith, founder of the Australian Geographic Society, and his blonde lady friend strode into view and, looking up, saw us careering down at them in a cloud of dust and pebbles.

'Hoi there!' a cheery grin and a wave, 'where are you headed, guys?' We came crashing to a halt in perfect unison. These two were the first foreigners we'd seen since leaving Darjeeling.

'Hello there,' I said in my best English, trying hard to look nonchalant about what we were doing. Not an easy task when you've just run fifteen sweat-soaked miles over the Himalayas, you're covered in dust and muck and your hair is sticking out wildly in all directions. 'We're heading up to Everest.'

'Great, and where have you come from?'

'Darjeeling.' I couldn't resist a smirk.

It was great to meet two people who spoke the same language as us. For ten days we had been speaking pidgin English/Nepali, using monosyllabics whenever possible, so the chance to put a few more words together with the two Australians was good.

Dick was also heading up to Everest but was disturbed by the amount of time his porters were taking and was coming back up the hill to try and find them. He was the organiser of an expedition to get Tim McCartnay Snape to the top of Everest. Tim is an Australian climber who, having climbed Everest once, was now trying to do it again. The story is that once he had got home and boasted to his 'mates' that he had climbed to the top of the biggest mountain in the world, one of the 'mates' told him that he'd cheated because he'd really started from half way up, i.e. at Base Camp and not at sea level. It's a load of nonsense of course, but Tim had taken this guy at his word and was now in the process of walking from under the sea at Calcutta up through India into Nepal, eventually to climb the mountain itself. What a nutter!

Dick and his lady friend, who must have been wearing the cleanest t-shirts in Nepal, were a great boost to our morale and we left them feeling that all our pain and effort was worthwhile after all.

Ten days ago we had set out from Darjeeling with just an inkling of what we were letting ourselves in for. Now, 250-odd miles further on, we felt like old hands. I knew now just what was possible, and I had pushed my daily expectation up by a quarter. Each day lasted thirteen hours and only one hour of stops was our average. It felt good to have got this far. Then the worst thing possible happened. Justin decided to stop.

His ankle had become too painful for him to continue and he thought it was on the verge of collapsing altogether. He could either carry on and wait for it to stop him completely, or rest while the

Justin's ankle becomes too painful for him to continue

opportunity presented itself and pray that it repaired. He had chosen the latter.

If he was going to rest up, then this was the time to do it. For our planned route meant that I could run up to Kala Pattar then back down to Lukla to meet him and we would go on to Kathmandu together. This would give him three days to rest the leg, which he hoped would be enough.

My mind was racing: alone again. I hate doing this sort of thing on my own. This had happened to me in China as well, when my partner's knee collapsed, and I had spent some very hard and lonely days out on my own in the desolate nothern Chinese deserts. When I run on my own, it's fine for a couple of days, then things begin to get very hard. There is no-one to talk to, no-one with whom to discuss the sights and sounds of the day, no-one to chivvy me on when I'm feeling down. I would have to be my own company and my own chivvier. But would Justin want to give up altogether if his ankle wasn't better in three days' time? I hoped, I prayed that he would not. I really did not fancy attempting the rest of this trip on my own.

Justin too felt sick about having to stop. He had proved a great deal to himself about himself over the past ten days and now all his hard-earned self-confidence teetered on one painful Achilles. He was going to miss the highest point of the trip up at the foot of Everest and was, therefore, understandably pissed off!

At Chaumrikharka, just below Lukla, we sheltered from the gathering storm under a covered gateway and went through the kit. I would take the camera and more film and give him much of the first aid kit in return. We shook hands and arranged to meet at this spot in three days' time. I turned north and headed up towards the biggest mountain in the world.

I suddenly felt very much alone. Even though Justin and I may not be the best of friends, I missed a companion already.

Having crossed over into the Dudh Kosi river valley, I have come into a different world, for the people and the buildings and the agriculture has changed. This is the Solu Khumbu area of Nepal and home to the people known as 'Sherpa'.

As the 'Himalayan Shuffle' takes over, I look around and drink in the new sights and sounds of this valley. The track is wide and well kept and a thousand footprints of both man and beast have flattened the dark brown soil. The sides of the valley are almost sheer, broken only by the occasional flat, upon which sit huddled villages of stone. Up there on the high slopes, the sun still shines, but down here in the bottom of the valley, the evening is already drawing in and the clouds are dropping down off the high peaks threatening to engulf me in their cold white shrouds. Down to my left the river roars a white torrent; never still, never calm, but always majestic.

The rivers in the Himalayas are a testimony to the power of nature. They have carved themselves a path through these magnificent mountains, tearing at the sides until the rock gives way and is carried down, as tiny particles, to be deposited eventually on the Indian plains. All the time the Himalayas are rising, some say by as much as three inches every year, and yet these tearing, frothing masses of water hold their own and cut even deeper into the rock.

I was running now up one of the most famous and visited of all Himalayan rivers, the Dudh Kosi or 'milk river', so named because of the white mica rock that fills its bed. These waters rose in the glaciers of the Everest *massif*, now only a few days away, and are eventually swallowed by the mighty Ganges.

On the banks live the Sherpa people. Round-faced, with eyes creased to thin slits, they are descended from Tibetans. Wandering over the high passes that surround Everest, they came down into the Solu Khumbu valley in the Middle Ages to trade. Now they are famous, not only for their portering and mountaineering skills but also for their enduring goodwill to strangers. They embrace the Buddhist philosphy of showing warmth and compassion to all animate creatures. While demanding little or nothing from other people, they are surprisingly demanding on themselves. For it is their portering skills that have enabled the Sherpa people to have a better standard of living than anyone I have seen in eastern Nepal. But portering demands great things from the body and I have never seen anyone work as hard as a Sherpa porter.

Today I have run past any number of small, barefoot and barrel-chested men, who, huffing and wheezing, lug enormous loads up and down these precipitous paths. A hundred pounds is common place, 200 pounds is possible. To put this into perspective, during the Falklands war the men of the Royal Marines carried hundred-pound packs across the islands. Some of these little men of Nepal are carrying double that and they are barefoot. Add to this the lack of oxygen at this altitude and you have one mighty tough race of people.

The most famous Sherpa of them all of course is Tenzing Norgay

Nepali baskets, loaded and ready for their owners

who, with Sir Edmund Hillary, climbed Mount Everest in 1953. Tenzing died just a few years ago and Justin and I had gone to see his grave at the Darjeeling Himalayan Mountaineering Institute before leaving on our run. Tenzing may be dead but his spirit lives on in Nepal, especially up here in his home valley, where physical toughness and the ability to keep going are part of everyday life.

There are a fair few white faces around too, for the 'Everest Trail' is on all the trekking brochures. In fact there are white faces, pink faces and brown faces. There are haggard faces, drawn and sick-looking faces, faces full of excitement, of achievement, faces that back home would say 'wow, you'll never guess where I've just been,' or 'God, I'm never ever doing that again.' There were Japanese dripping with cameras, Americans armed with guide books and Israelis attired in the latest pastel mountaineering fashions. Yes, I was well and truly on the 'Everest Trail'.

It felt strange at first for I had been alone with my partner in the vastness of the Himalayas for ten days and had got used to it. Now, suddenly, I was sharing my wilderness with other foreigners and for a while I felt indignation about their very presence in my mountains. But this was foolishness of course and I would just have to get used to it.

I had been running for what seemed like ages but was in fact only an hour. Contouring the valley, climbing steadily all the time, the track zigged and zagged and I was beginning to imagine that I was on a road to nowhere. My target was the little community of Phakding, but I felt sure it was moving away from me as fast as I was running towards it. Surely it would be round the next bend, or maybe the one after that . . . and so it went on. At last, after a thousand zigs and a thousand and one zags, the whitewashed buildings of Phakding appeared. Straddling both sides of a small river, this place was a sight for sore eyes and a welcome for weary legs. I stooped to enter a smart, two-storey building with a glistening new corrugated iron roof. The sign outside said, 'Welcome to Tashi Taki Lodge. Apple pie served here. You look good.'

Well, I certainly did not 'look good'. Dirty and smelly and sticky with sweat, I collapsed onto a wooden bench and let the relief of stopping wash over me. The bench had a thin cushion over it and I could feel the softness through my increasingly bony body. I was in heaven.

'Hello, do you want a bed?' I sat up, embarrassed at my

forwardness in coming in and flopping down unannounced. A very pretty young Tibetan face was peering at me from round the door to another room.

'Ah, er yes, yes please,' I stammered, suddenly and rather stupidly ashamed of my disgusting appearance. The young girl showed not the slightest concern about the state of her new customer. She was about twenty and wore her hair tied back severely behind her head to hang in a long plait down her back. She really was strikingly pretty and for a moment I was caught off-guard.

I followed her up the wooden steps to the next floor and, having decided that the rooms were too expensive for me, settled for a dormitory bed. In fact I could have had five dormitory beds if I had wanted, for there was no-one else staying. There, in front of me, was my idea of heaven. Five fluffy blue-and-white-striped mattresses. The promise of all this comfort was almost too much to bear. I chose a corner bed, plonked another mattress on top of the one I already had, and collapsed.

'The crawling glaciers pierce me with the spears
Of their moon freezing crystals, the bright chains
Eat with their burning cold into my bones.'
  P. B. Shelley

Chapter 8

GODDESS
MOTHER OF THE EARTH

I woke to clear skies, a fresh early morning breeze, boiled eggs, Tibetan bread and steaming black tea.

Shouldering my pack and waving a 'cheerio' to the young Tibetan proprietress, I was away by six o'clock. Crossing and recrossing the river on swinging bridges, one of which was at least sixty feet above the swirling waters, I passed porters galore. Sherpa people, men and women, staggering under enormous loads up to their capital Namche Bazaar. Tomorrow was Saturday and that means market day in Namche. People come from all around the area, both lowlanders and highlanders, to buy and sell and gossip. It is an exchange of lowland goods for highland goods for the lowlanders carry up rice and corn and return with potatoes and wool and other goods that would otherwise be unavailable to them in the different climate down the valley.

I cross the river by yet another swing bridge and then climb steeply up the last 2,000 feet to Namche Bazaar itself. The track is steep and slippery and the snow lies in melting patches. I am feeling strong and my legs carry me quickly up the hill. Many of the Sherpa porters are barefoot and seem to think nothing of plodding through the snow, the weight of their loads holding them firmly to the ground and pushing their feet through the cold covering up to their ankles. It is those porters coming down who have more of a problem, for they slip and slide continually and the strain on their necks from keeping their loads steady must be excruciating. All of them carry a T-shaped stick which acts both as walking stick and rest platform for their loads. Indeed the only time I really see these Sherpas' faces is when they stand upright in small groups by the side of the track, their heavy baskets resting on the T-stick as they take a breather. Then one of their number will make a short whistle and they bend forward in unison, taking the strain onto their heads and necks and plodding on up the slope, bent over with the weight of their loads.

As I climb higher and higher, the Dudh Kosi valley opens up behind me. The fir-clad slopes are topped with black, rocky crags that disappear into the fast-descending clouds. It has begun to snow. Thick flakes soon coat the ground in a soft, freezing, white blanket and I stop for a second to change into my thermals. It has suddenly got very cold, the coldest of the trip so far, and the wind starts to freeze the ends of my fingers.

I round a corner in the track and Namche Bazaar appears through the gloom. The tight group of houses sit squashed into the small hillside bowl. The snow is pouring down in a continuous sheet, blotting out the light and turning the village into rather a forbidding-looking place. No one is about, they are all sheltering from the weather, and there is an eerie quiet.

I creep up through the mud and slush and find refuge in a small lodge, where a steaming bowl of *tsampa* porridge soon warms and revives. The porridge is a traditional Nepali meal – roasted barley flour with hot tea poured over it – and is eaten by the kilo by porters who need bulk and carbohydrate to maintain their energy reserves. Suitably refreshed and warmed if rather bloated, I decided to continue on up the valley to try and reach Tengboche at 12,400 feet. Here the risks were piling up for I was in danger of getting altitude sickness.

Every year, people die of altitude sickness. The lack of oxygen in the thin air above 10,000 feet can cause coma and eventually death as the bloodstream and thus the brain are starved of oxygen. This dangerous condition can creep up on athlete or armchair sportsman alike, for everyone is affected in different ways.

A trekker below Phakding had told me about a young girl who had gone into a coma in the middle of the night up at a village called Pheriche, several miles up this valley. Her tent-mate had woken to her partner's incomprehensible ramblings and had fetched the New Zealand doctor who was based in the village for the trekking months. The girl was in danger of dying right there in the tent. The doctor immediately ordered for her to be taken down. Some Sherpa men took it in turns to carry her inert body on their backs, over the snow- and ice-covered rock in the black of night for several miles down the valley, to a point 1,500 vertical feet below

'He travels the fastest who travels alone.'
Rudyard Kipling

Ed runs alone up towards Kala Pattar

Pheriche. The girl recovered. The Sherpas had saved her life. What started out as a relatively simple trekking holiday had turned into a nightmare drama of life and death.

I did not want the same thing to happen to me and yet the very nature of the expedition added to the possibility that I too could succumb to the altitude. I knew the symptoms; shortness of breath, loss of appetite, headache, lethargy, and I knew that if I succumbed to these then I would have to turn back. But reaching Kala Pattar was everything. This was the highest point of the trip and I must not fail.

All the other trekkers I had met were taking an extra day of rest at Namche to acclimatise, then one day at Tengboche, and another two days at Pheriche before ascending towards Everest. That's seven days altogether from Namche Bazaar to Kala Pattar. I planned to try it in two.

I was nervous as hell while climbing up out of Namche Bazaar. The snow had eased slightly and the ground crunched softly underfoot. As I saw it, I should be well enough acclimatised up to about 15,000 feet and after that, well, I would just have to wait and see. I resolved to use the American adage 'Listen to your body', to watch out for any of the symptoms of altitude sickness. I was also drinking a lot of fluid, for the cold air soon dries out the body and that can help bring on the sickness as well. I was now above the danger zone, pushing at the altitude without the suggested rests for acclimatisation, and feeling very aware of the risks I was taking. So far I felt fine.

The snow-covered track continued up the side of the valley and, having climbed high above Namche, it stayed almost level, contouring in and out of the sides of the slope. Away and up to my right was the 21,000-foot mountain of Tramserku, but I knew this only by looking at my map, for the clouds obscured all views. My world had shrunk to a one-hundred-metre-long bubble in the mist. I felt lonely and exposed.

I slipped past a few porters and nearly bumped into a small train of yaks coming round a steep corner by a large commemorative mound of stones called a *chorten*. The leading animal raised its nose off the ground and glared at me with baleful eyes. Its grey, shaggy coat of long hair was covered with snow, and on its back an enormous load of filled rough sacks and bundles was held in place by a knot of rope. I leapt to the side of the track, narrowly avoiding the yak's long curved horns, and stood there as the train passed me by. In the Himalayas, when confronted by animals coming the other way, it is always prudent to stand on the inside of the track, the danger being that if you stand on the outside, then one shove from the belligerent beast would send you tumbling out over the edge of the precipice to disappear forever. Behind the train came two Sherpas, a man and his small son, both wrapped in heavy wool cloth to protect them from the weather. What a harsh life these two must lead, to-ing and fro-ing with yaks and goods up at these altitudes. I did not envy their lot.

Then I was running again, down to Phunki Tenga, crossing the Dudh Kosi for the last time as it turns north-west. I was heading north-east up the Imja River and soon climbing steeply through a beautiful dark green pine forest up towards the famous monastery at Tengboche. I planned to rest here and acclimatise overnight before pushing on and up tomorrow.

The lodge at Tengboche is full of trekkers, all heading up towards Everest. They are dressed to the eyeballs in thick duvet jackets, tough walking boots and warm trousers, so when I staggered in wearing my Reebok running shoes, thin thermal gear, t-shirt and funny long shorts, I caused a few raised eyebrows. I sat quietly in a corner writing my diary and drinking copious amounts of tea.

Later, the snow stopped falling and a fresh wind blew the clouds off the mountains. The sun appeared and lit up the most majestic views I have ever seen. I got my first view of the highest mountain in the world. From here I looked out over the Nuptse ridge and up to the top pyramid of Everest itself. Not much snow on the top but huge clouds blowing in spiralling patterns from the summit. All around me were snowy giants. Everest, Nuptse, Lhotse, the long finger of Ama Dablam piercing the sky, snow and ice defying gravity, clinging to the sheer sides. My eyes roamed over ice fields, glaciers, cornices, rock buttresses and knife-edge ridges. The word 'Himalaya' is the Nepalese name for these mountains and it means 'abode of snow', for in this beautiful, frozen wilderness live their gods, magnificent, mysterious, and all-powerful. I wondered at the fantastic forces that have pushed this rocky mass up into the sky. It dwarfed me and I stood in awe.

On this small ridge that is Tengboche, the yaks were munching on hay, carried up on their own backs; a space was being cleared of snow for someone to put up a tent; a young monk, only a boy really, skated down the slope on a couple of short lengths of pipe, (Torvill and Dean eat your heart out); and the ruined monastery stood broken and derelict on the hillock opposite the lodge.

The monastery was built in 1916, although the ridge of Tengboche was regarded as sacred long before that. Then on 19 January 1989 a curtain caught fire and the whole structure went up in flames. Many paintings and statues were recovered in time but much was lost. The cost of repair is estimated at US$800,000 which money has now been raised and I heard that Sir Edmund Hillary is coming here on 7 April to lay the first stone of the new monastery. The resident monks now live in tiny stone shelters and in the ruins of the building itself. It amazed me that these people can survive up here in this cold, for even though the sun was now out, a cold wind froze my cheeks and searched out any opening in my clothing.

The next morning I was up and away before anyone else had stirred. Plodding through the fresh snow, mine were the only footprints and the way was unclear. It was cold and I wore all my clothing bar the duvet jacket. There was no sound, the air was still and my feet softly crunched the snow underfoot. A musk deer crept out of the spindly wood and down onto the track in front of me. I froze, delighted at the sight but not daring to move for fear of scaring it away. It sniffed at the air and paused, one forefoot poised above the other. Then in a flash and a flurry of snow, it was gone.

I kept the pace very slow and steady, all the time listening to how my body was feeling, searching for signs of altitude sickness. But none came. I was peeing every half-hour, a colourless liquid, which meant I wasn't dehydrated.

I carry on though Pangboche, the first Sherpa capital, now just a tiny collection of grey stone buildings, and on up to Pheriche at 13,600 feet. It is a cold desolate place, in a wide flat valley. The clouds hang over the surrounding mountains so that only the lower slopes are visible, and at Pheriche you can feel quite cut off from the rest of the world. The village consists of just a smattering of tiny stone huts, all just one storey high and, with the snow covering everything, it almost disappears from view as you come up onto the valley floor. A main thoroughfare cuts a straight line through the huts, and mud and slush make my feet wet and cold and dirty. The place reminds me of a frozen spaghetti western setting, where a man's life is cheap and only the roughest can survive. But the small, hardy folk who live here bear no resemblance to Clint Eastwood or Henry Fonda. These people are real and they are survivors.

In a tiny, dark and very cold hut, I talked with a man called Pasang Sherpa as he cooked up some Tibetan bread for us both. We were huddled close by the small wood stove, feet and hands stretched out to the warmth. My running shoes were sopping wet and my toes felt rather blue, but the orange flame crackled and spat and warmed.

Pasang had lived up here for all of his thirty years. In winter he went south to work down in the Dudh Kosi valley but at the first sign of spring he would return home again. He farmed potatoes and hired himself out as a porter. Sometimes he would land a job taking yak trains around the surrounding villages, collecting goods to be sold at Namche Bazaar. Now, he ran his tiny lodge and cooked for foreign trekkers. 'No people here now,' he said. 'More come in summer. I do much cooking then.'

As soon as I could feel my feet again, I decided to try going on. The next set of huts is at Dughla, another 1,000 vertical feet up. I will be pushing my luck a bit, but I feel fine so far. With no headache or giddiness, and permanent hunger, I have no symptoms at all.

It was a slow, plodding climb up to Dughla. Feeling rather light-headed I concentrated on breathing slowly and deeply and not making any fast or jerky movements. I walked with pigeon steps up the steep snow slope, finally topping a ridge, and there in front of me lay the rocky moraine of the Khumbu glacier, a huge bundle of boulders, 1,000 feet high, the whole scene covered in snow and ice. This boulder mountain has been formed by the action of the glacier pushing the rock before it as it descends. Dughla sits, almost hidden, right at the foot of this mass of rock. There are just three stone huts and I enter the middle one. For the rest of that afternoon and evening I sit huddled by the fire, trying to dry my socks out and keep warm. The Tibetan lady, who stays here all spring and summer, had only arrived a few days ago for the trekking season. She cooked up the best Tibetan bread I have ever tasted and kept a flask of hot sweet tea permanently filled.

As soon as it grew dark I retired to my sleeping bag to get a good kip before the big day to the top tomorrow. It was as cold as I've ever known it and I pulled the drawstring of my sleeping bag tight, leaving just my nose poking out of a tiny hole. My breath left trails of vapour in the freezing air.

Huge, white, rolling waves crashed onto the shore and sent plumes of water high into the air. The air was full of the sound of water rushing back over the rocks, then again the gathering thunder of another big wave. I was caught up in the maelstrom of swirling water. It grabbed at my clothing and dragged me down. I was drowning, unable to breathe, sucking in water, mouthfuls of water, no air, my throat so tight, the noise of thunder again, gathering until it filled my ears. Don't let me drown, don't let me drown!

Suddenly I was sitting bolt upright, tearing at my sleeping bag, trying desperately to get out. The dream left me as the cold of the

Himalayas slapped my exposed face. I had turned right round inside my sleeping bag and had blocked my air hole and now I sucked in lung-fulls of air. But the 'shooshing' sounds in my ears were real enough and I was dying for a pee. Throwing the constricting bag from me I dragged on my frozen shoes and raced out into the night. Just in time. I stood there in the snow, a black sky lit with thousands of stars that shone off the snow slopes all around. The jumbled mass of rock that was the Khumbu moraine towered threateningly in the dark.

Then my world started to swing violently. The rushing sound in my ears built and built and filled my head. I was swaying where I stood, trying desperately not to fall over while peeing but I had no control. I stumbled around. The ground and the sky became one, racing round, tumbling, racing. This is crazy. The altitude: I've come too high. I'm going to die up here. I couldn't stand still, there was nothing to lean on, my legs were like jelly and I stumbled and fell into the snow on my side, wetting myself in the process. For a few seconds the swinging sensation continued then stopped. The sky and the ground separated and my head cleared. I felt terribly scared. The cold wetness of where I had urinated over myself began to chill me to consciousness and I crawled slowly to my knees and then stood up. I was OK. Still short of breath but OK, and I concentrated on breathing deeply and slowly.

Back in the sleeping bag I lay still and felt terribly alone. I think I had got short of breath because I had twisted in the bag, then a mad dash to get outside for a pee, getting up too quickly, sent my head reeling. Now, with slow movements and deep deliberate breaths, I felt better, the headache went and my ears had stopped roaring. I was going to be alright. I must not fail. I must get to the top tomorrow, but I was scared. Not for the first time this trip, I offered up a little prayer.

The rest of the night passed slowly, but as the first rays of light broke the nighttime gloom I slipped gently out of my sleeping bag and joined the Tibetan lady as she lit the fire in the stove. My shoes were like ice and my fingers stung with the cold as I tied the laces. My trousers had dried during the night and I was grateful for the cold as it prevented any smell. I would have to wash at the first opportunity.

I was hungry, which was a good sign, and soon the lady had a small pile of fried Tibetan bread ready. I shovelled down as much as I could. Today was a big day and I would need all the energy I could get. Six cups of tea later (no water this morning for it had frozen solid in my water bottle) I headed out into bright sunshine and a brilliant blue sky that set off the white and black of the land. I donned my glasses to prevent snow blindness and set off up the hill towards Lobuche, apparently two hours away.

I was there after one hour, having climbed up through the western edge of the moraine. The views opened up as I climbed and I exulted at being alone in the middle of the biggest mountains in the world, in difficult conditions and pushing myself and my luck to the limit. This was exciting indeed.

Lobuche was another couple of stone shelters. The snow had been blown up against the sides of the huts and it gave them a sort of half-buried look. I expected anyone inside to be the same, only half-alive, but I found Gary Ball and his Sherpa porters, very much alive. Gary is a New Zealander and an accomplished climber. He has been a member of two previous Everest expeditions and this therefore was his third attempt to get to the top. He was actually leading two expeditions, one to climb the mountain and another to clean up the Base Camp area.

Countless expeditions to Everest have left their rubbish in the snows at the foot of the Khumbu ice fall. This rubbish has built up to a disturbing level and back in New Zealand Sir Edmund Hillary had put out a distress call for the place to be cleaned up. Gary Ball had taken up the challenge and had organised a party of young people to follow his own climbing expedition up to the Base Camp. They were going to clean up the area and have all the rubbish carried down on the backs of yaks.

I drank another four cups of tea here at Lobuche, wished Gary and his porters good luck and disappeared ever upwards, heading for Gorak Shep, last stop before Kala Pattar. The track, now barely discernible, twists and turns over the rocky, snow-covered moraine. Here I saw unbelievable views of the Khumbu glacier with its jumble of ice, snow and blue cavernous crevasses. The wind had whipped itself up and blew cold on my back, pushing me on. I was going to make it. Again, the two-hour trek took me just one hour and I clambered down off the jumbled moraine onto the tiny flat plateau of Gorak Shep.

Then, at last, I was climbing the final hill of Kala Pattar, the translation of which is 'Black rock', for the summit is just that. I was

Ed on Kala Pattar, the highest point of the trip at 17,900 feet

feeling on top of the world. My legs powered up the near vertical south slope, breath rasping in my throat, last night's scare long forgotten in the exhilaration of achieving my goal. I was on the top after just one hour, at the highest point of the whole trip and at a new altitude record for me of 17,700 feet. My diary of the time tells its own story.

All around me are glaciers, jagged peaks, ice towers, crevasses, and snowy cornices clinging to the slopes like drips of icing on the side of a cake. I can list off the famous mountains, mountains that as a child I had dreamed of seeing for real and now here I am in the centre of them all. The finger of Ama Dabalam; Pumori, shaped by ice into a perfect pyramid; the jagged ridge of Nuptse and behind, Lhotse; but towering above them all is the massive bulk of Everest. The Tibetan name for this, the greatest of all mountains is 'Chomolungma', Goddess Mother of the Earth. Almost clear of snow on its western wall, a huge plume of cloud racing from its summit. This mountain creates its own weather. I feel so small and insignificant in all this grandeur and yet inside I feel like a giant. What a place to be.

The wind was now biting cold and whipped at any exposed skin. My face froze and my fingers went numb. I suddenly felt tired and realised the danger that I was in. I took some photographs then ran at full tilt back down the way I had come. The wind was now in my face and I plunged in true fell-running style down the slope. My thin shorts and thermal underwear were not enough of a match for the freezing wind and my privates began to ache painfully as they froze. There was only one thing for it. I shoved my hand down my shorts, grasped their contents and ran down clutching my marital gear, trying desperately to keep it warm. I went flying past a couple of trekkers coming up and got some very strange looks. A crazed Englishman with a huge grin, whooping with glee as he flies down the hill, dressed in baggy tartan shorts and Reeboks with his hand shoved down his trousers. No-one would ever believe them.

Back down at Gorak Shep, I filled up on more tea, checked that everything was still in place inside my shorts and ran on down the valley. It was midday and I had to get down below Dughla to be safe from the altitude.

The next five hours were the worst of the trip so far. The snow clouds came in and the temperature dropped, as did my morale. Retracing steps, I became more and more tired. My left ankle began to ache and my lungs hurt. The villages of the last two days passed by in a blur. Lobuche, Dughla, Periche and at last Pangboche where I collapsed into my sleeping bag by six o'clock, absolutely exhausted. Moving at speed in this cold, up at this altitude had really taken it out of me. Roll on the warmth of the valleys. Kathmandu here we come.

By the end of the next day I was really very tired indeed. My legs just were not interested and the ups and downs drained all the energy from me. The miles dragged by and I longed to be running with someone again. I also had a nasty chest infection brewing. Tengboche, Namche Bazaar, and Phakding passed by, then finally I arrived at the lodge where Justin was staying.

We met and shook hands, all smiles. I was tired and sore and very pleased to see him. Now everything would be alright again. Justin was also pleased to see me and had been getting very bored over the last few days. We chatted as I shovelled down a large plateful of noodles, and then he hit me with it . . .

'My ankle is still bad, Ed. I really don't know if I can go on.'

I had a flash of anger, then a feeling of being let down. How dare his bloody ankle not be better? But this was stupid. I was knackered and had been so looking forward to running with him again that it hadn't even occurred to me that he might not be better.

'What do you want to do?' I asked. I wanted to cry with frustration.

'Well I'm not bloody well going home, that's for sure,' he said. Was this the Justin that I knew? 'The thing is,' he continued, 'that if I run with you to Kathmandu, then my ankle could go altogether, and then you'd be alone for the rest of the trip. But if I fly from Lukla, then I can meet you in Kathmandu. By then, surely, this bloody thing will have mended itself.'

He was absolutely right. I really did not want to have to attempt the rest of this trip on my own. The last three days had been hard enough, but another eighty-five or ninety days alone could break me altogether. No, he was right. A lesser man would have disappeared off home at this stage and it is a tribute to Justin's loyalty and sense of purpose that he stuck with it and with me. He was bitterly disappointed, but was determined to take the long term view.

We say goodbye for the second time in three days and then I'm on my own again. From now on I have no choice in this trip. If I'm injured, tough! I'll just have to keep going somehow. The days ahead to Kathmandu will be hard but I'll get there. It's just so damn difficult on your own. If only I wasn't so tired. What lies ahead is a crazed dash over 170 miles of the Himalayas to Kathmandu. The route is against the grain of the land and there are six major ridges to climb. I am going to follow the trekking route out to Jiri, which sits at the end of the road, then cut off onto the old trading paths, before hitting the road again at Lamosangu, forty-five miles from Kathmandu. Leah arrives on 2 April. That gives me about seven days.

Chapter 9

THE ABYSS OF SELF PITY

Today is Day Fifteen of the run and despite an aching chest, sore throat, phlegm and wind, somehow I'm still going forward. What a moaner I'm becoming though. I have a saying for this type of behaviour; 'falling into the abyss of self pity'. At the moment I feel as if I'm teetering on the edge of that abyss.

Today, I started off attacking the hills with venom, but that's no way to survive. You have to live with the hills and not compete with them. I relaxed, steadied down, and the miles began to flow by. Chutok La pass, Phuiyan, Kharikhola, Jubing (here a trekker, a stunning blonde with wonderfully long legs, grinned at me as I ran by), then up, up and more up, over the Tragsindho La pass at 10,000 feet. What a climb! It seemed to go on forever, but in fact lasted for just two-and-a-half hours. Very muddy at the top by the prayer flags and as I was coming down I took a spectacular tumble and got covered in mud. Things were really going well. The snow snowed, the cough coughed and the legs, well they somehow just kept going. At Ringmo I wolfed down a plate of hot, sticky noodles and an apple pancake (apple orchards around here apparently), then dropped to the Beri River and headed out for Sallung.

The countryside had changed already. I had left the precipitous cliffs and towering snowy peaks far behind. The hills here were smaller, rounder, more populated, less forested. The people were well used to foreigners, for I was on the tourist trail. I must admit to preferring the remoter parts of the country. The people are so much more natural. Here it's a bit money-grabbing.

After Sallung, the track led steadily up and round the spur. I startled a mountain goat. Great muscley shoulders bulging with effort as it ran headlong down the near-vertical slope, leaped across the track in one bound not sixty feet in front of me and crashed through the undergrowth on the other side. The sheer speed of the thing on that slope amazed me. If only my legs had that sort of power, I'd be in Kathmandu tomorrow.

I jogged on, past a tiny cheese factory high up on the hill, where hard yak's cheese is sold to passing trekkers, then down to the riverside village of Junbesi. There is a large school here, founded by Sir Edmund Hillary, and hordes of chattering children are coming out just as I arrive. Up the tiny cobbled path, through the houses, past a large white Buddhist commemorative *chorten* to the lodge which I had seen as I descended on the other side of the river.

Here, while sipping tea and glugging on a Fanta orange drink I met an American couple, Ron and Mandy, who recognised me from Tengboche. They were heading down from Everest as I was heading up. I must have been travelling pretty fast if I'd caught up with them already. If only I had felt fit and fast. I just felt rather dead instead. Still the cough would go soon and I'd be right as rain, I hoped.

From Junbesi, I shuffled on up the valley towards the Lamjura pass, at 11,500 feet the highest of the six I had to cross before Kathmandu. Time and light began to fail me, not to mention knackered limbs and a grumbling stomach. I clambered up through trees dripping with mosses and lichen and rocky outcrops pouring with snow-melt, rhododendrons splashed bits of red and pink onto the dark canopy of the wood and the bright colours were a comfort as I trudged upwards in the driving snow and fading light.

At last Tragdogbuk swam into view through the gathering gloom. Just two wooden buildings and a cheery group of Sherpa ladies squatting by the stove, trying to keep warm.

I am now ensconced in one of the buildings, alone with a number of Sherpa porters who are all heading up to the pass as well. They pore over my map and watch closely as I write my diary. They are such smiling and gentle people, I'd share anything with them and certainly don't mind giving them maps and diaries to look at. They treat them carefully and always hand them back with a little bow of the head and a smile. A kerosene lamp lights the interior and nearly sets light to the whole lodge. Towers of flame as one of the girls lit the thing. Back home we'd have panicked and called the fire brigade. Here, hardened hands pass through the flames with no feeling and the lodge is saved as the blaze is put out. Nepali newspapers have been pasted all around the walls. Photos of family

and pictures of glossy Kathmandu models look down on the
chattering porters, and dotted triangles of yak's butter form
religious symbols above the doorway. *Daal baat* awaits and
tomorrow I head for Jiri then on to meet Leah in Kathmandu.

Day Sixteen passed in a blur. I was up at the crack of dawn as
usual. Hacking cough and painful bottom. I had the feeling I had
some sort of infection down there. I couldn't wipe it when I needed
to; it was just too painful. A good wash was in order as soon as
possible.

Within an hour I had topped the Lamjura pass. Snow and ice
cloaked the ground and the going was slippery and treacherous.
From the top, which was still in shadow as the sun had not yet risen
high enough, I looked back at the Everest Massif, glistening white
and jagged. It was already bathed in sunlight and, standing alone
and high on my ridge now far off to the west it was as if it was lit up
especially for me.

I gazed for a while and thought back over the events of the past
few days, then turned my back and set off for Kathmandu. A long,
rough and rocky, knee-jarring descent brought me 6,000 feet down
to Kenja village, nestling in a tight valley by the Likhu River. The
snows were now high above and I was back in the warm country
again. The sun was hot on my head and tiny birds of many different
colours darted from tree to bush to rock as I ran past. The river
splashed loudly and crystal clear over its rock-strewn bed; a
fisherman squatted on the bank, his rod held lazily in one hand;
small fields, carved flat from the hillsides, marched up the slopes;
and the urgent cries of the ploughmen carried down to me on the
breeze, as they urged their beasts onwards. A group of brightly
dressed ladies were washing clothes in the river, slapping the
sagging material on stones and laying out the bright, clean articles
on boulders to dry in the sun.

Another long and steep climb, sweat pouring from every pore in
my body, to the scattered village of Bhandar, where I sat under a
tree for a while, chomping on glucose biscuits and gulping at my
water bottle.

By seven o'clock that evening I had crossed another two small
passes, competed in an unacknowledged race with two Sherpa
porters carrying empty baskets to Jiri and passed by *Mani*-stone
walls galore. Each stone is inscribed with the Tibetan Buddhist

Mani Walls on high passes carrying prayers to the Gods

chant of *Om Mani Padme Um*, offering up a prayer to the Gods. The inscription translated literally means, 'Hail to the Jewel in the Lotus', but there are a host of other religious and philosophical meanings as well.

Jiri came and went in a blast of twentieth century. This was the end of the road and the first time I had seen vehicles for twelve days. I never like coming back to a road after periods of absence. In the hills the people are friendly and natural and I can relax, but as soon as I come close to a road, peoples' natures change. Money becomes more important and there's always someone trying to screw me for more than something's worth. There is a rudeness as well that I just did not see in those who live in remote areas. I passed straight through Jiri, stopping only to grab a cup of hot *chai*.

Most foreigners will travel here by bus from Kathmandu then walk in to Everest from here. Some will fly out again from Lukla, others will walk out to Jiri again and catch a bus back to Kathmandu. This means that the old footpath to Kathmandu from here should be devoid of foreigners, which suits me down to the ground.

About a mile out of the town, the road bends sharply round to the north and I cut onto a tiny track. It leads me through clumps of bamboo and along the side of a steep spur before dropping down to the community of Sikri. It is growing dark and I am keen to get inside tonight. The community is very rural, untouched by the road which passes by several miles away up the hill. No tourists, no lodges and little food. At the first house I come to, a mud-built, two-storey structure with wooden shutters and a thatched roof, the father of the small family 'ums' and 'ahs' for a few minutes, obviously a little unsure of this dishevelled stranger with dirty brown teeth and funny shorts, then invites me in. I duck inside the low doorway and into a dark, smoke-filled but warm room. It is very bare. Just a mud floor and a few straw mats. By one wall is a dip in the floor for the fire and a large metal tripod straddles the flames. The rice is on the boil. The man has two wives, as his first wife produced four children, all of whom died as babies. His second wife has given him two sons and two daughters, and now they all live side-by-side in this one house.

I sleep out on the porch, for inside there simply is not enough room. Above my head, swallows fly in and out of their tiny mud nests under the eaves and, in a hole in the wall, a wasps' nest buzzes quietly. I must have run twenty-five miles today and perhaps as much as thirty yesterday and my legs twitch involuntarily as I lie there looking up at the half-moon gathering brightness in the fading light.

That night was not a night I want to repeat in a hurry. I slept only fitfully on the mat in the porch of the mud house, and I'm pretty exhausted now. My legs ache and my whole body cries out at me to stop. Getting up at half past five every morning is becoming increasingly difficult. I go around in a bit of a daze. This stage on my own is turning out to be one long haze of pain and frustration. If only it wasn't so hard. Today was up, then down, then a long, long traverse along a massive, sprawling spur. The path was not obvious at all and I got extremely frustrated whenever I lost it. The mist hung low and it began to rain, and I hobbled along, now feeling very sorry for myself. There seemed to be no end to this up and down. Always the next ridge, always the other path. I was now clinging to the sides of the 'abyss of self pity' by my fingernails, part of me telling me to let go and another part willing me to hang on, to keep going.

Twice on the way to Shera, I lost the track altogether, stumbling over boulders and rivers, almost crying with frustration. I cursed everyone and everything.

The villages today were very backward and poor. Farming communities that hadn't changed the way they did things for centuries. There was very little food around and I did not eat all day. My stomach grumbled for sustenance and I tried to stave off the pangs by drinking a lot of water to fill myself up. My right knee began to ache and I had diarrhoea . . . again!

The final climb of the day, a leg-aching, knee-groaning stumble up a hill that just wouldn't end, took me to Muldi on the road again. As I topped the ridge, far, far away was the Everest Massif, bathed in the orange evening light. I was so tired after the climb and this view, I knew, would be the last I'd see of Everest this trip. I saluted these magnificent mountains and vowed to return some day. I had made it over the final one of the six major ridges and this, coupled with the view, put me on a high. I felt a great burst of happiness well up inside me and strode purposefully into Muldi, singing 'Rule Britannia' at the top of my voice.

Muldi had nothing to offer but a cold *daal baat*, served to me by people who really couldn't care less. After a sudden downpour that stopped almost as soon as it had started, I set off in the dark down towards Lamosangu. As I trudged down at a steady Himalayan shuffle, the evening was warm and I enjoyed the peace and the easy running. The stars came out, a silver moon hung in the sky, bathing my surroundings in a ghostly hue, and the road became a shadowy, silver-grey snake that stretched away endlessly. I trotted on into the night, 'thumb up bum and mind in neutral', as they say in the Marines, my legs churning up the miles.

Sleep came late into the night when a young family took me in and I slept on a tiny wooden bed, my feet sticking out over the end. Outside the cardboard door, water buffalo snorted and munched on hay. The minute my head touched the wooden pillow, I was asleep. Day Eighteen: I must have made thirty-five miles yesterday and now I'm well and truly exhausted. My legs are running out of power and I ache all over. My right knee is so sore that I stagger around for five minutes every time I get up. What am I doing out here?

The sheer, endless frustration of the thing got to me today. I came down off the ridge on a track, heading for a little place on the Kathmandu road called Balephi. Coming steeply down, my knees crunching away at every step, I must have taken just one crucial wrong turning, for down at the Sun Kosi River there seemed no way across. Hot, sweating and thoroughly pissed off, I staggered along the boulder-strewn riverbank in the heat, gazing up at the road only a few metres away on the other side of the river. There was no way across, apart from swimming, which would have been stupid. A lone Nepali fisherman pointed me back up the way I had come and everything just broke at once. I felt the hot sting of tears of frustration in my eyes and I completely lost my rag, screaming obscenities at the sky and feeling that it was all so unfair. I was trying so hard. Why should I get it so horribly wrong? I stormed back up the tiny track, up, up back the way I had already come. Life could not have been worse. I had let go of the edge and had plunged into the abyss at last. All I could think of was Kathmandu and the promise of comfort and rest, but it seemed to be moving away from me all the time.

Two hours later I was on the road, having crossed by a footbridge upstream, and then the rest of the day began. Endless twisting road, all tarmacked, and hot; so hot. Sweat poured from me and I drank Fantas, tea and water to stave off heat stroke.

This horrible road, it just goes on and on. My right knee is playing up badly now and is throbbing even when I sit down. I stretch continuously, trying to soothe the injury. The road goes on. As I

Below:
Ed (left) and Justin
Left:
Nepali man carrying a filing cabinet

Overleaf:
The Everest Massif

Far Left Above:
Nepali man drinking from a gourd

Far Left Below: A Nepali tractor in the
rice paddies of East Nepal

Left: *Daal Baat* (rice and lentils).
Our staple diet for 85 days

Below: A Kiranti lady of east Nepal
beautifully adorned

Right: The yak.
Bad tempered beast of burden and a
cross between a cow and a Rottweiler
Below Left:
High altitute adventurers
Far Right: Sherpa village scene

Ed at Gorak shep with the mountainous hulk of Pumori in the background

pass by the side of the Sun Kosi River, a kingfisher with a bright red beak and fluorescent blue back perches on a twig and watches as I jog by. The road goes on. Egrets flap lazily over the water and a cormorant races over the river making waves in an effort to get airborne, a ferret ferrets around in the bushes and a hummingbird floats on invisible wings. The road goes on. As I pass through more and more villages, the children come begging, 'Give me rupees, hello monkey, hello, hello, hello, hello.' Their high-pitched cries make me irritable again and I swear softly whenever I hear their persistent little voices. The road goes on. Up, up, twisting from gully to spur to gully to spur, up eventually to a tourist resort. Tiny red brick houses perched on a hill overlooking the majesty of the Himalayas. Pasty-faced and fat tourists dripping with cameras stagger down the steps of their luxury coaches, waddle up to the restaurant where a brass band plays 'For He's a Jolly Good Fellow' and 'Auld Lang Syne', then stagger down to the coach again, which whisks them back to their Kathmandu hotel, where they collapse, exhausted after a day's work. The road goes on.

At last at Dhulikhel, town on the hill, I stop and check in at the unexpectedly posh 'shoes off' hotel for foreigners at thirty rupees for a bed. My knee hurts and at least there's only tomorrow to do before I can rest it for a couple of days. Chips, fried chicken, apple pie and banana pancake does wonders for the morale. But that road, I hate it.

Day Nineteen. Only twenty miles to go. Twenty miles. Back home I could run that in two hours, but now the twenty miles may as well be two hundred. My knee is terribly painful, my bottom hurts (I suspect piles), and I generally feel very run down.

The road winds up and down small hills and valleys, through tiny, dirty roadside communities. Old ladies gathering water in large metal jugs; young girls balancing bundles on their hips; a dead dog on the road, just run over and still twitching, the crows already gathering; stalls selling hot milk tea from grimy glasses and piles of battered bread rolls crawling with flies. The same flies buzz around my lips as I glug on a bottle of Fanta and little kiddies with snotty faces gaze with wide-eyed wonder. An old man twists back the head of the chicken he holds between his knees, and violently hacks at its neck with his knife. The blood drips hot and crimson into a dish and is carried off by the man's tiny son. The chicken's legs are still kicking. It's a harsh living. Men sit or stand around at the roadside, waiting for a bus, buying goat's milk, drinking tea or just passing time. They gather at the tea stall and watch me drink. Their toothless grins, laughing eyes and gentle manner make me smile. I rest my head back against the smoke-blackened hut wall and, for a moment, forget about everything. Then a truck belching black fumes roars by, shaking the shack on its foundations, and I wake from my reverie, rise unsteadily to my feet, slowly stretch my aching limbs and hobble on down this endless road.

The villages become more regular, with more people, more traffic, more noise, and then at last there it is, away in the distant, smoky mist . . . Kathmandu. Just a sprawling collection of low buildings, but for me a true metropolis and a long-awaited rest. Justin will be there waiting for me, as will a hot shower, waffles for breakfast and my Leah. My knee is so very painful now and I cannot run. The elastic bandage supports it to some extent, but I wince with pain and try singing to take my mind off it. I hobble painfully through the suburbs, past the clock tower and up the main Janpath road. Turning into the Thamel area of the city, at last I am at the door of the Garuda Hotel, where Justin is staying.

I am filthy, unshaven, tired and in some pain but the warm welcome from the Garuda staff, who know us from our time here in February, makes it all seem worthwhile. Not for me the photo flashes of publicity, the handshakes from dignitaries, the dinners and cocktail parties. I arrive unannounced but victorious. I have made the run from Kala Pattar to Kathmandu in just under six days and I have proved to myself that I can do it. The only reward I want is a welcome from Justin and a chance to have a wash and put my feet up. I'm here at last and the memories, the painful memories, fade very quickly.

Chapter 10

A TOWN
WALLOWING IN TURMOIL

I met up with Justin again and he looked well rested and confident about his ankle. He was sure it was better and dying to get going again. He'd seen the doctor and had taken a course of anti-inflammatory pills and used a cold balm. I started up the same treatment for my knee.

Kathmandu was a bustling metropolis and now the trekking season was fast approaching, there were a lot of tourists. Everyone dresses up in the latest outdoor gear, all very fashionable, and then they tart themselves up for the night. It has become the place to be seen if you're cool and trendy. This really is not my scene. I can't stand the trendier-than-thou feeling that has embedded itself in the young tourists here. Anyway, I was not planning to leave my hotel room, for this was my rest-stop and rest was what I intended to do.

It never works out as you plan it, of course. There was too much to do and, as ever, too little time to do it. I had to get my shorts repaired for I had worn several holes in the bum; I also had an extra 'warm' patch stitched into the front of the shorts, in an effort to prevent the 'freezing-willy' condition that had nearly robbed me of children up on Kala Pattar. I wrote thirty-seven postcards to friends, family and sponsors back home; checked my money supply; wrote an article for the newspapers and ate vast quantities of anything that came my way.

Leah arrived on 2 April. She looked slim, fit and well, and as beautiful as ever. She arrived with a large envelope full of letters from home and a lot of chocolate. I can't resist chocolate. The two of us and Justin had dinner together and chatted long into the night. But while I rested, Kathmandu was wallowing in turmoil. The opposition to the ruling party had called for the people to rise up against their current oppressors and set up a democracy. The students from the universities had taken up the call for change. There were regular general strikes and riots and a nightmare curfew, imposed by the army, turned the capital into a ghost town.

A sense of danger pervades the air. People are angry. It's a far cry from the peacefulness of East Nepal. We heard no inkling of the troubles out there. But here revolution is in everyone's mind and 'freedom' and 'democracy' are the words on everyone's lips. In back street bars and dingy cafés, small groups gather and talk in hushed but animated tones. Then, when the time is right, they spill out on to the streets demanding freedom of choice and a democratic government.

At the moment the Kingdom of Nepal is ruled totally by its monarchy, headed by King Birendra Shaha. The King and his Queen have surrounded themselves with relatives, whom they have placed in all the key positions of power. Thus they maintain total control of the country. There are reports of corruption on a massive scale; of diverting of funds to private bank accounts; and of new businesses closing down because they had refused to hand over free shares to the royal family. But I got the impression that the dissatisfaction was centred mainly in Kathmandu and a few of the larger towns in Nepal. Out in the hills, I had heard nothing of all this unrest. It was the university- and college-educated people who were demanding the change. To the average Nepali peasant, the King can do no wrong. Indeed he is regarded almost as a god, for Nepal is a Hindu state and King Birendra is the head of that state and is therefore much revered. He has also done much good for the country via charity. Since Nepal was opened up to the rest of the world in 1951, after the overthrow of the Ranas dynasty, much foreign aid has been secured by the new ruling family. At that time Nepal had no monetary capital, no resources and no technology: it was a country living in the Middle Ages. But now the nation has a very open mind to development and is building a manufacturing and service industrial base. It is happening very slowly, but it is happening.

But years ago, the King made a mistake. In order to try and ease implementation of his reforms, he created the 'Panchayat' system. This gave the King absolute power, as well as banning any other political activity. Nepal had become a dictatorship.

It was this lack of freedom of choice and alleged corruption, coupled with the recent changes in eastern Europe, that sparked off the dissatisfaction amongst the people once again. The King had responded with force. While we were in Kathmandu, pickets of police and soldiers roamed the streets. They were in riot gear, wearing flak jackets and helmets and carrying long wooden batons. I looked at their faces. Many of them were just boys and as the shutters of the shops came crashing down for yet another general strike, they looked terribly vulnerable.

A number of riots took place while we were in Kathmandu. As soon as one starts, a buzz spreads like wildfire through the city. The soldiers and police suddenly look very alert and scared. Figures rush off through the streets to join the riot and an air of frightened expectancy fills the air. Reports come to us of people being killed, the army opening fire, the streets being full of tear gas, many people being arrested without charge.

Leah and I walked back to the hotel very late that night, at around eleven o'clock. It was pitch black, for the street lights had been turned off by the authorities. It was curfew. Small groups of armed riot-control police patrolled the tiny narrow lanes, and torchlight swung through the dark, confusing us in the windy streets. We were glad to reach the hotel, for the night was menacing and threatening indeed.

But the inner turmoil of Nepal affected foreigners very little. We could come and go almost as usual. There were some deaths of foreigners reported, but these people had been too inquisitive for their own good. They had joined one of the riots to take photographs and, when the police opened fire, they had been among those killed. Other people we talked to were affected only by cancellation of planes and buses, by the nighttime curfew and by the regular general strikes. Out in the hills, life was going on as usual, the peasants being more concerned with just surviving than with the struggle for power.

We also met Mark Waltham of Intermediate Technology. Mark was based out here in Kathmandu and, as a qualified engineer, was helping set up micro-hydro projects all over Nepal. The recent troubles seemed to affect his job very little, for most of the work took place out in remote villages. He was immensely positive about what he was doing and showed us round his partner's metal workshop. The workshop is owned and run by a Mr Akalman, the Nepali gentleman who first came up with the idea of micro-hydro electric schemes.

It was Mr Akalman who came to Intermediate Technology for

help nearly ten years ago, and that help now arrives in the form of knowledge and expertise as well as goods. In the workshop, sparks fly, wax castings melt, metal is hammered, bent, shaved and filed until eventually three new turbines appear each year.

Between the two of them, Mr Akalman and Mark Waltham, a tremendous amount is achieved, for there are now micro-hydro schemes all over Nepal, helping people to improve their lives. One

Mark Waltham (left) of Intermediate Technology and Mr Akalman. The drive and brains behind micro-hydro-electricity in Nepal

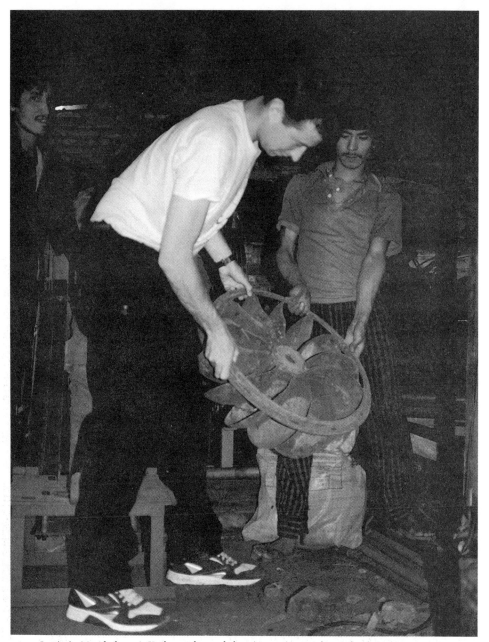

Justin in Mr Akalman's Kathmandu workshop inspecting a pelton wheel

such scheme operates at Muktinath, north of Annapurna and on our route. This scheme uses any excess electricity to heat water for hot showers in the street. The showers are sold to trekkers and the village now earns some extra income.

Mark is also involved in helping the Nepalis to design and build more efficient pots for cooking on electric. Even house-insulation techniques and training lie in his sphere as well, for when the household starts to use electricity instead of wood for cooking, there is no smoke and thus no need for holes in the roof. But how to keep the heat in by using traditional building materials, and preferably less of them? This is one of the other questions that I.T. are addressing. A host of projects, all low-tech and highly practical, will be up and running soon enough.

I said a tearful goodbye to my Leah outside her hotel. Meeting so briefly after nearly two months feels really strange and now she's gone again, already I want her back. She is off to do her own trek and to have her own adventures and I am off to have mine.

We parted and she didn't stop waving until I'd turned the corner of the road, a lonely figure in the distance, hands waving in the air. I turned away with a lump in my throat. I won't see her again for another three months.

Justin and I had stayed for two-and-a-half days in Kathmandu. It was time well spent for when we came to leave I felt a little more refreshed. My knee was still sore; not as bad as it had been on the run into the city, but still sore. I had it strapped tightly for support, but I must admit I was feeling terribly worried and frustrated about it all. I had a reputation to live up to now, so stopping was out of the question.

Justin seems a whole lot happier about the whole trip. His ankle is mended and he is raring to go. He had some good, positive letters from home about what he was doing and that seemed to have made all the difference, for it's a changed Justin who jogs out of Kathmandu with me this morning of 3 April. He exclaims at the beauty of things, laughs more easily and generally seems far more relaxed. I hope this state of affairs continues, for it will make life that much more pleasant for me if I don't have to keep worrying about cheering him up all the time.

We are heading north-west for Trisuli Bazaar and then directly westwards out towards Manaslu and Annapurna, our next big mountains.

Just out of town, we have already slowed to a painful walk. The way is uphill for nearly twenty miles and my knee is still sore. We tried running for a while, zig-zagging round the long switchback bends, but the muscle on my knee contracted painfully at every step and I had to walk. This was obviously very frustrating for Justin, who was full of bounce. But he was patient and stuck with me. My injury is muscular and should get better in time and ideally, with rest. Unfortunately I have room for neither so the bloody thing will just have to get better on its own. 'Oh well,' I keep telling myself, 'it wasn't meant to be easy, was it?'

At the top of the climb, we cut down off the road at a tiny place called Ranipauna, having purchased a couple of packets of biscuits and some dried noodles for the night, in case we cannot get food. The track cuts north, down into the valley and should save us a fair few miles of bone-jarring road. It's cold and windy, and there's a lot of rain about. I must admit to feeling rather depressed. I miss Leah already and my aching knee worries me sick.

We look back down the way we have come and far away is the misty Kathmandu valley. Stage One is now over. We have proved that we can do it and there's only 1,600 miles to go.

'You have heard the beat of the off-shore wind
And the thresh of the deep-sea rain
You have heard the song – how long? how long?
Pull out on the trail again.'
    Rudyard Kipling

Chapter 11

THE STUBBER

The track was a deep rut in the sandy brown soil, eroded by water and centuries of plodding feet. We added our own plodding feet to it and dropped down into the valley. Stopping at the tiny village of Chadwide, perched on the side of the slope, we found shelter with a small family. Justin took the mat on the dusty earth floor and I took the mat on the bed. A broken shelf clung to the wall above my head. A few dusty old bottles and an empty packet of fags sat on top. A small black puppy poked its head around the door and chickens pecked and clucked around the bare room. The shutters were open and I could see that the rain had stopped. The sun set a pale orange and the myriad of hills faded shades of soft blue in the dimming of night. It was good to be away from the hustle and bustle of Kathmandu and back into the peace of the hills.

At first light, we steal quietly out of the house and stumble off down the hill and onto the flat valley bottom. Rice paddies glisten wetly in the early morning sun and the tiny track skirts the very edge of the fields, so that at times it is like running on a tightrope. If we fall off, the safety net is a wet and muddy paddy.

Passing one small hut, we hear the whirring sound of machinery. Inside, two rice-threshing machines are hammering away, with ten-foot-long fan belts spinning crazily and men moving about amongst the rice husks, machine oil and moving machinery with studied care. The safety standards are non-existent and I wonder how many fingers have been lost or bones broken. I had always ignored the hard bits in my rice but perhaps from now on I'll check a little closer . . . just in case! The whole lot is run by water, which is channelled from the stream into a large pipe above the hut, drops down and drives a small water wheel, which in turn drives the fan belts, and thus the machinery. A simple and highly efficient source of power.

We run on, my knee feeling better today. I have strapped it very tightly indeed and I keep the bandage wet so as to counteract any swelling. We lose the path a number of times and end up wading through the myriad of streams and one wide river. We may as well have jumped into the paddy fields first thing this morning. Anyway, only our feet are wet and, as we used to say to the young people who came up on the Outward Bound course, 'Your skin is waterproof, so why worry?'

Hitting the road again at Trisuli Bazaar, we pass an army barracks where Gurkha soldiers are being put through their paces on the parade ground. Excellent precision drill is to be seen as they march and turn and come to an immaculate halt in a cloud of dust. Justin and I march past in step, playing the fool, and salute as we pass the gates. Big white-toothed grins appear on the soldiers' faces as they stand to attention being bawled out by a sergeant, who has his back to us, and a group of corporals salute us back, laughing away either at our little joke or at the appalling state of our drill.

Trisuli Bazaar was as we remembered it from our visit in February, when we had arrived on the bus on our way up to the Langtang valley for training. It was dirty, noisy, and unfriendly. We passed straight through. Off the road once more, we wouldn't touch tarmac again until we came to the far western border of Nepal, perhaps three or four weeks away. It was a wonderful prospect.

We are running now in the ancient, well trodden trade route to the old capital of Gorkha. The Gorkha tribe, led by a man named Prithvi Narayan Shaha, conquered all the other small principalities in Nepal in 1769 and founded the 'Kingdom' of Nepal. The Shaha dynasty established themselves as a strong monarchy and it is the very same family that still holds power today, over 220 years later, indeed King Birendra is a direct descendant of Prithvi Narayan Shaha. The Gorkha expansion was halted by the British, who were so impressed by the fighting qualities of the Gorkha people that they allowed the Kingdom to remain independent. Thus did the Shaha dynasty survive. The British also recruited many of the tribe's fighting men to join the British Army and that tradition continues today in the Gurkha regiment.

Running on up the dirt track in a wide valley, we are surrounded by fields of wheat and barley and corn. There are many small, dirty villages with wooden balconied mud houses, chickens, cows and screaming kids. People are travelling in both directions all the time. We climb steadily up through this agriculturally rich valley, over a small pass, then down through ever-steepening spurs and staggered terraces.

At the ridgetop village of Tharpu, we have to squeeze past a long procession of brightly dressed men and women, all heading back home after attending a religious ceremony close to the village. They have been celebrating the reincarnation of the Hindu deity Vishnu, the Preserver. The ladies are a colourful splash of reds and yellows, with gleaming ear- and nose-rings. Some of them carry umbrellas to shade themselves from the sun.

We ran for thirty miles today and eventually stopped at Sundhara Bazaar, where water buffalo grazed lazily on leaves, and tiny, near-naked kiddies yell and tumble around in the dirt. There are no hotels or inns or anything of that sort out here, so we ask around to see if there is somewhere we can sleep. An old man with a wispy grey moustache and untidy little beard shows us to a room with two beds, and a huge bundle of dirty bedding. To us, this is heaven. We lay out the bedding to form a mattress and put the sleeping bags on top. After we have eaten I stand outside in the dark and listen to the sounds of the night. Bullfrogs croak from hidden pools, fireflies glitter like tiny beacons in the trees (a magical sight), other insects buzz away gently and a half moon is reflected blue in the paddy fields that surrounded the village. Leah's lonely waving figure filled my mind and for the first time this trip I felt homesick.

Midday the next day, twenty-four days after leaving Darjeeling, finds us sitting in a little *chai* hut in Arughat Bazaar on the Buri Gandaki River. It is hot and we are dirty and sweating. We gorge on noodles and greasy cups of sweet tea. A man, sitting on the floor, is making samozas and we wonder if, as he's pinching the pastry closed, he has trapped any of the thousands of flies that land on everything.

Justin is scratching between mouthfuls of noodles. Last night was awful, with mosquitoes dive-bombing our ears and gorging themselves on our blood, and bed bugs attacking my feet and crawling up my legs whenever I stuck them out of the sleeping bag in an effort to keep cool. My bites don't seem to bother me now, but poor old Justin is scratching and itching away at the large welts that have appeared all over his body. The flies are settling on everything.

I can feel them now, crawling over my knees and calves. When we eat, we always take a quick look at the spoonful of food before plunging it into our mouths. I've eaten two flies this trip and Justin has eaten four. I keep telling him, 'This is not a competition I want to enter.'

'4–2, 4–2,' I get back in football song tones.

'Lovely bit of extra protein though.'

'I think I'm going to be sick.'

We've nicknamed these *chai* houses, 'Nepali Little Chefs', for they always seem to appear in the most unexpected places. Tea is a cheap and easy drink to make and is sold all over Nepal. The mixture of water, tea leaves, sugar and goat's milk is boiled up in a saucepan, then sieved into a tiny glass or metal cup. The cups do not have handles and can only be two-thirds filled, otherwise the drinker burns his fingers. It sounds like a good little ruse to me, but not once in Nepal have I seen a cup with a handle. Back home I've got a pint-sized 'Three Peaks' mug for tea. You could probably get four or five of these little cups into my one mug.

I dip my finger into the scalding liquid and clean the rim of the grimy glass, lift it to my lips and slurp quietly, thinking of my large mug back home. It's strange sometimes the things that one misses while away.

We ran on, knees and ankles holding together well, following a winding river bed upstream. We crossed and recrossed the small river until it became a stream, then just a trickle. As we climbed higher the stream bed got more and more narrow and twisty. We must have been running at least twice the necessary distance, and our legs began to ache with the effort of leaping from boulder to boulder. At intervals we came across 'Little Chefs', tiny leaf-thatched dwellings made from rocks and fallen branches. Some of them were empty and disused, but others contained fellow Nepalese travellers, who smiled and waved as we jogged by, tripping over the loose rocks.

Topping the ridge at Kanchok village, Justin cooled himself down at the village tap and I had to make an emergency dash for a toilet. There was no actual toilet as such, there very rarely was in Nepal. We just went wherever we could. My Western upbringing demands a little privacy when I'm doing ablutions, but sometimes, when the foreign food has played yet another nasty trick on my bowels, I have to throw caution to the wind and just get on with it. This was one of those occasions.

Then we were running again, at speed, down a rock-strewn river bed, heading for the Dharandi Khola. We had decided to bypass Gorkha, not only because it is at the end of the road and we didn't like roadside towns, but also because we thought we'd found a quicker route. The running was rough but much more fun. We had yet another small piece of paper with a few scribbled names, only two of which were on our map, and we were going to take a chance at finding people on route who could help us with directions.

Running down the stream bed, Justin is in front keeping a good, steady pace and I am settled in behind him, plodding away in neutral. I coin a new Himalayan Run phrase, 'The Stubber.' A 'stubber' is a medium-sized rock that lies for hundreds of years in the same place, then after all that time it suddenly decides to jump out just as we are coming along and whack the end of our toes. The 'stubber' packs a powerful punch.

The next scribbled village is called Nibble. Understandably a village with a name like that did not get away with it for too long. The rhyme went something like this:

Two runners were having a quibble
On which is the best way to Nibble
Said the ex-Royal Marine
From what info I've gleaned
Girls in Nibble sure wiggle and giggle.

We sang our childish but rather fun little ditty as we ran and it helped to take our minds off tired limbs and aching feet. Then another 'stubber' whacked the end of my toes and I shut up.

We crossed the Dhorandi River balancing on a few haphazardly placed logs, inching across over the hungry waters, not daring to look down, then ran on south down the river bank past banana trees and small fields. At Chorkate, we cut west again and two hours later climbed the final few steps to Khoplang. We had got lost again, twice. I hate getting lost. It's always when we are not concentrating or when we haven't bothered to take the compass out to check. Then, too late, we find ourselves crashing around in the dry brush, or clambering up a slope only to have to descend again. Getting lost is a waste of time and energy and always makes us annoyed and irritable.

Khoplang is a tiny, clean hill village. Carved wooden balconies, mud walls, red-tiled and thatched roofs, a paved central path; tiny kiddies racing around, genitalia and snot flying everywhere; an old lady with a face furrowed with wrinkles sits out on a mat under her porch and rocks herself gently; a large grey dog trots by proudly holding a cow's leg in its jaws. A small pipe protrudes from the side of a muddy bank and spatters water onto a round stone underneath and the water has worn a saucer shape into the top of it. This is a village living in the Middle Ages.

Half past five the next morning finds two trans-Himalayan runners climbing stiffly out of their sleeping bags. We spent some time stretching, easing out sore muscles, much to the amusement of several buffalo, a cow, three goats and a sleepy little girl picking her nose. A couple of glugs on the water bottle and we were away.

We've both settled into this run now and although we have only come three days from Kathmandu it feels a lot longer. We've come eighty-five odd miles in those three days and, apart from a little early morning stiffness, both of us are feeling good. It is terribly satisfying to plot our continued progress on our map, the scale of which is 1:1,550,000, which means that we move about an inch per day. There are approximately sixteen inches left to the border with India.

We are running through tiny communities just waking to the day. The fire is crackling in the stove, with tea and *tsampa* porridge on the boil. Sitting in their porches, people watch us with sleep-filled eyes as we shuffle on by.

After two hours of non-stop running, the village of Luitel Bhanjyang opens up to a paved but muddy street and a few *dobi* houses with corrugated roofs and stained wooden shutters. We are already well attuned to the day and are sweating buckets, the legs thumping with effort and the body crying out for grub. But the rest of the village is only just stirring and the villagers wave, shout or just stare as we appear, a bedraggled and knackered-looking duo.

Sitting on tiny stools with a group of middle-aged men drinking their first *chai* of the day, we chat in pidgin Nepali/English about the route. We are now used to getting the information we need and can make ourselves understood well enough. The route-finding in this expedition is all-important for, if we are to achieve the one-hundred-day target, then we must give ourselves the best chance. But what with neither of us speaking enough Nepali to converse, it's always a bit of a battle. We had been advised back home that when asking for directions, always ask an 'open' question. A Nepali in general will be keen to please, so if he has a choice of saying 'yes' or 'no', he will choose 'yes' even if he knows the answer is 'no'.

There is no malicious intent at all, but a Nepali will just expect you to be happier if he says what he thinks you want to hear.

We tend to ask the open question then wait for the small crowd that usually gathers around us to babble animatedly, discussing which is the best route. We let them chatter away, for out of it usually comes the quickest route from A to B. Once all the names are down on paper, we try to get some idea of how many hours it takes them to walk between one village and another. Then after that an idea of whether we climb, descend or traverse between points. The latter information is useful but can sometimes be quite wrong. I once got some directions from a young man who knew just the odd word of English. I found out the route and the times, then tried to get the nature of the terrain. I used my forearm as a hill, which could be heading up or down as I moved my hand. I got the directions and we set off, expecting to go downhill for three hours. We went up for six. The young man had read my arm from hand to elbow and I was reading it from elbow to hand. Directions were prone to misunderstandings, but we seemed to manage well enough and after all, we were getting there in the end.

We filled up on tea, then headed west for Chepeghat then Tarukghat Bazaar on the Marsyangdi River. It took us two-and-a-half hours, but we ran all the way, taking it in turns to lead, skimming over the rock and hard-packed earth.

At one point, two young lads of about sixteen or seventeen ran with us for about twenty minutes, and they did well.

'I play volleyball and my friend does the shot-putt,' said one. 'What do you do?'

How could I explain fully what we were doing? 'We run,' I said.

It was fun running along with these two, a bit like having an escort. People shouted and waved and grinned as we ran by. Occasionally we passed groups of small schoolkids and they would dash along behind us, shrieking with delight and rolling onto the ground as their tiny flip-flops caught in tree roots on the path. We ran with wide smiles on our faces, leaping over rocks and flying over the ground with apparent ease, laughing aloud at the fun of it all.

Through the trees and dappled shadows, over tinkling streams, round fields of corn and bushes of bamboo, past munching buffalo and sleeping dogs, nothing could stop us today. Painful knees and ankles were forgotten, and the two of us ran on together, eating up the miles and revelling in the feeling of being alive and fit in the hills.

At Turukghat Bazaar we hit the 'Pancake Trail'. This was our second and last planned detour. We could legitimately keep heading west from here on our traverse of the range, but to the north is the massive bulk of the Annapurna range and west of that is the Kali Gandaki valley, the deepest in the world. These sights are too good to miss, so from here we will head north on the 'Annapurna Circuit', aiming to cross the Thorung La pass at 17,300 feet and run down through the Kali Gandaki before heading out into remote western Nepal.

The 'Annapurna Circuit' is popular with trekkers and has attracted many enterprising Nepalis. They are of a different tribal group than those in eastern Nepal. Here we met Tamang and Gurung peoples as well as a scattering of Magar. These people are mainly recognisable by their ladies' ear- and nose-rings. The ear-rings, made of lightweight gold, are often three inches in diameter. There are two types of nose ring, one piercing the centre of the nose, and the other the left nostril. The rings are shaped into a variety of designs, such as Christmas trees, shields, stars, studs, triangles. All of them are made of gold. I have heard that the goldsmith fits the rings and that thus only he can take them off.

Many of these people have set up lodges along the route around the Annapurna Massif and have adapted their menus to the Western taste over the years. The joke is that you can get a pancake anywhere on this trail, hence the 'Pancake Trail'.

Justin and I had arrived early in the season, so we were hoping that there were not too many tourists around. However, even if there were, it was unlikely we would see many of them due to the vastness of the area.

Chapter 12

THE GIVER OF LIFE

It is midday in Tarukghat and we gobble down our first food of the day: mountains of rice, potatoes, *daal* and buffalo meat with an omelette thrown in for good measure, then shuffle up onto the wide track that will take us to Besisahar.

We are going like trains and roar through the village one-and-a-half hours later, stopping only briefly for chapatis with jam. The wide track comes to an end and we are on a narrow, twisting footpath again, heading up the west side of the Marsyandi river. The river is a huge, violent surge thundering down the valley, cutting an enormous gorge, whose sides disappear up into a world of ice and snow thousands of feet above our heads. Fir trees paint the slopes a rich green and we run on a brown carpet of needles. Tiny flowers fleck the ground with pastel blues and yellows, and fallen branches, now rotting and enveloped in a shroud of dark green moss, litter the side of the track. But all the time the river commands attention, its rushing noise softening and crescendoing as we twist and turn along the path, sometimes climbing up and away, then twisting back down to its banks. We will follow this river upstream, eventually to its source and beyond. But for the next couple of days it will be our guide through these formidable mountains.

We've run around thirty-five miles today and have stopped at the Gurung village of Khundi high up above the river, where a full body wash under a trickle of water from a carefully balanced bamboo stalk revives aching limbs. It's been a good day.

Twenty-six days of running (actually twenty-four if you take off the two days spent in Kathmandu) and I can still hare along at true fell-running pace. We are both going far too fast but, what the heck, it's fun and we are enjoying our fitness. From Khudi we are racing north, upriver, our legs carrying us up all but the steepest of slopes. We pass several small groups of trekkers. Some English youngsters give themselves away by muttering, 'Too keen!' to us as we pant past and another group say, 'You are running'. There's no answer to that.

Sometimes the sides of this enormous valley close in like a giant vice, and the river disappears far below as we climb up over one rocky outcrop after another. White waterfalls plunge down hundreds of feet to disappear in a spray of foam into the main river.

Landscape east of Annapurna at the Marsyangdi River

Justin is at last really enjoying this trip. He's even exclaiming out loud at the beauty of the place and whooping and shouting with glee as we bounce and skim over the rugged terrain. Our fitness has evened right out now and we are running better than ever. Since Kathmandu we have relaxed a little, now that we know just what is possible. This new found confidence, especially on my partner's part, has gelled us into a better team. The unlikely duo are slowly coming together.

In our excitement we pushed it too hard this morning and so the last five miles into the village of Danaqu seemed endless. We suddenly have no energy left. In the lodge there is a group of nine ladies sitting in a semi-circle round the fire. They are obviously all good friends for they chatter away, laughing and giggling like schoolgirls. Justin and I sit in a corner, feeling like intruders. The ladies have taken their shoes off and left them scattered about the room. The fire glows orange in the mud stove and pots and pans sit on top, their contents sizzling. It is dark in here and the light from the fire reflects flickering flames off the pans and the ladies' metal teacups. Tomorrow our target is Manang, the last stop before the Thorong La, gateway to western Nepal.

We woke to a clear day and sunshine; what a change from yesterday's cloud, mist and rain. We walked to begin with as our legs felt very heavy, then began to run slowly. Some of the bounce had gone due to yesterday's excesses.

After an hour or so we have climbed high enough up this valley to have almost continuous views of the white snowy peaks all around. The jungle-like forest has disappeared entirely and fir trees abound.

Sun lights up hidden gullies and sugary cornices high above, and the wet from last night's rain glistens on leaves and track alike. Snow lies in melting patches and a roaring spout of white water showers us in spray as it gushes from the rock above our heads. We run by on a tiny wooden bridge, gasping at the power of the thing as it disappears into the black pool below our feet. The main river has turned a murky grey-green colour, the result of the gritty glacial water that tumbles down from the high peaks.

The track forces its way up the valley, crossing and recrossing the river on long, shaky swing bridges. Sometimes it becomes a three-sided tunnel where it has been cut right into the rock. The work involved in building these tunnels must be enormous. It's an eerie feeling, like being almost swallowed by the land.

We are running directly across a cliff face. Over the edge the rock drops sheer a hundred feet to the river, and roots of grasses clinging to the face hang over the opening, dripping water and giving a false sense of protection from the drop.

The villages we pass are slate-grey blocks of tiny houses, flat roofs covered with chopped wood as a supply for the stove. Wisps of smoke curl up into the tree-tops. At one point an avalanche has deposited tons of debris over the track, and it is a strange feeling running along on pine needles, then suddenly having to clamber up over jumbled blocks of snow and ice. But the very fact that this avalanche is here at all makes us nervous and we run on, taking anxious glances at the huge cliffs of ice and snow up above. I occupy my mind by making contingency plans as we are running along. If I spot an overhanging cornice or a dodgy-looking snow field I make a mental plan to dive this way or run that way if it should crack loose and start falling towards us.

At the sleepy village of Chame we feed on noodles and omelettes and sit staring wide-eyed at Manaslu, one of our big mountains. We traversed it as we came into Tarukghat a couple of days ago but this is the best view of it yet. It stands framed by the darker, nearer hills, a giant dwarfing everything around it.

At Kodo, there is a police post and for the first time since the Everest region, we have to show our permits. The official, a green-uniformed Nepali policeman with slicked-back hair and a star on each shoulder, looks at the permits, then holds them out for me.

'You cannot go on.'

'What do you mean I cannot go on?' I say, hackles immediately rising.

'Where do you want to go?' he asks.

'Manang, then over the Thorung La. We are on an expedition.'

'You cannot go.' He pushes the permits back at me, sits back in his chair and turns his head away. The interview is obviously over.

I have encountered this sort of petty officialdom many times in my short life so far, but I have still not got used to it. Every time this happens I can't help feeling intense anger and frustration. I would have loved to have grabbed this guy by his lapels and shaken some sense into him. I bite my lip and say quietly through clenched teeth, 'Please tell me why we cannot go on.'

'You cannot.' A vague gesture for me to disappear.

'Yes, but why?' teeth grating.

He snatches the permits back off me, opens them up and points at the line entitled 'Route of Trekking.' 'Manang is not listed here. You cannot go.'

If he says 'You cannot go' one more time I'm going to brain him, I think.

I ask as politely as I am able, not an easy task when this petty official is holding the expedition in the palm of his hand, to fetch his superior. This guy is ruining a great day.

The superior arrives. He is older, has two stars on each shoulder and a wide, gentle smile on his face.

I explain what Justin and I are doing and that we have been given special permission by Mr Singh of the Nepal Immigration Department to pass right through Nepal. The reason why Manang is not written on the permit is that we are passing through a hundred different places from east to west and there simply is not room to write them all on the card. If he looked carefully, he would see Gorkha and Jomsom then Beni were on there. The only route between these towns is through Manang and over the pass.

The superior nods kindly while I talk and then turns and berates his younger officer for not letting us go through. We are ushered by with much smiling, nodding, and 'Namaste-ing,' and the crisis is over.

I glare at the young man who has been so belligerent and when we shake hands to say goodbye I squeeze as hard as I can. He has unwittingly played with my emotions, sending my feelings bouncing up and down like a yo-yo and I don't thank him for it.

In 1988 in China during my run along the Great Wall, my partner Dave Wightman and I had been plagued by officialdom throughout the difficult journey. Indeed we had been arrested six times altogether, but that's another story. Needless to say, an opinion about petty officialdom has been formed in my mind, and I find it increasingly hard to be patient when some self-important official decides to throw his tiny bit of power around.

We left the police post fuming but relieved and ran on. Within an hour we topped a ridge and the most fabulous view appeared. The incident was promptly forgotten.

From our vantage point by a large cairn, from which sprouted Tibetan prayer flags flapping lazily in the breeze, we gazed out at another world. The Annapurna mountain range rears massively to the south, fir trees cling to the snowy lower slopes, rock bands stretch horizontally across the snow cornices and at the base of the mountains, jagged sandstone pinnacles stick skywards, their cracks and gullies eroded by thousands of years of wind and rain. It was a scene straight out of the 'Lost World'.

'Will you look at that,' said Justin. He was standing gazing out at the valley, hands on hips, with sweat dribbling down off his face and dripping onto the rocks.

'What's that film with dinosaurs and a burrowing machine or something?' I queried.

'Journey to the Centre of the Earth.' Justin knew every film there was to know and usually most of the scripts as well.

'It's just like the scenes in that film. I think I saw Doug McClure just now, chasing a Tyrannosaurus Rex.'

'And there's Raquel Welch in a skimpy fur bikini.'

'Over here, Raquel!' I hailed to the empty space in front of us.

Justin on the 'Pancake Trail'. The lost valley beckons

'Actually, no, come to think of it, Raquel Welch was in another film, *The Lost World* or something like that.'

'Who cares!'

We stopped goofing around for a second and just gazed out in wonder at the snow, rock, trees, waterfalls and icy mountains. Justin turned and said slowly and with much gravity, 'I think this is the most beautiful sight I've ever seen.'

'Except me, you old bugger. Come on.'

We ran down and into the lost world.

We are now traversing the Annapurna Massif. There are five major peaks in this range, all now to the south, and we will traverse each of them in the next few days. I gaze up at the vast expanses of snow and ice clinging to what look like vertical slopes. The mountains are a huge cake, haphazardly drowned in icing. Snow cornices drip sugary lumps from ledges and ridges, fluted ice columns glisten blue and white and jagged, and gleaming snow slopes threaten to slide off their rocky anchor at any second. Annapurna means 'Giver of Life' for the melt from its snows feeds the valleys. The crops, the people, the animals and plants are all supplied with life-giving water. But up there on the cold mountain itself there can be no life, for nothing could survive up there for long. It is a remote and unfriendly world and although man may climb the mountain, he is always a visitor and when he leaves, the mountain remains as wild as ever.

That is what I love about the mountains. They will never be conquered. Man has tamed so much of the Earth in his short life on the planet, but Annapurna and Everest and Kanjenjunga and many others of the great mountains of the world will remain forever unconquerable, unchangeable proof of nature's total domination of us all.

Justin and I jog slowly into Manang at 11,300 feet. We are up at altitude again and set to head up for the pass tomorrow. The area is dry and arid, not unlike the Peruvian Altiplano the two of us had experienced together in 1985. The similarity ends, though, as soon as you look up. Then the mountains fill your mind. The houses are small, grey, flat-topped affairs, huddled closely together, with notched-log ladders leading up to a small door. The narrow alleys shut out the light and mud and snow piles up in slushy messes that make the feet wet and cold. We have come nearly twenty-five

Traversing Annapurna, the 'Giver of Life'

miles today and will stop here in a lodge for the night to stock up for a big push tomorrow.

This is the make-or-break day. We are heading for the Thorong La, the 17,300 foot pass that is the northern gateway to western Nepal. If we fail, we face a ten-day detour back round the south of the Annapurna peaks and that means we might not make the hundred-day target.

I've heard so many conflicting stories from the trekkers we've passed that now I just ignore them. Some say the pass is open, some say it's closed, others tell us of huge avalanches and still others warn of ferocious winds. The one consistency is that everyone has told us it is quite impossible to go over the pass in our time scale and that we are sure to die of altitude sickness if we go up any further. These other trekkers are bloody good at handing out advice unrequested. As Justin says, I'm sure they mean well, but it gets my goat. I'm afraid anyone who starts harping on about what we should or shouldn't be doing gets the sharp end of my tongue. I'm fed up with it. But looking at it from a trekker's point of view, we are travelling about three or four times as far as them every day. So to someone who's flown out from Paris or Tel Aviv a couple of days ago, what we are doing probably looks pretty crazy. I suppose when I think of it, it is, but because we are already well acclimatised, we can do it.

We dragged ourselves out of our warm sleeping bags at half past four this morning, an hour earlier than usual, in order to give ourselves a good start. 'Up with the sparrow's fart again,' said Justin, and this brought on a smile. It was still dark and the mountains all around were flooded with an eerie blue moonlight. The Annapurna range to the south rears massively from the valley floor, dwarfing everything else. It's cold and the tips of my fingers feel like ice as I don my still-wet running shoes. We shovel down last night's stodgy Tibetan bread and finish off the black tea in the Thermos. Then, buttoned up against the cold, we set off.

Creeping in the semi-darkness through the tiny muddy lanes of Manang, taking countless wrong turnings, we are saved by early morning ladies carrying empty baskets. I stop three times (yes, three times) to empty my bowels. A little brown dog joins us and we name him 'Mongrel Sherpa' as he seems to be showing us the way. Climbing up the right-hand side of the valley, the terrain is dry, beigy-brown and barren. Mongrel Sherpa pauses at each rise and looks back at us as if to say, 'Come on then!' He is a good companion. We are walking all day today because of the altitude. The pass is very high and remote, and a long way away from anywhere. The thin air can bring on altitude sickness quickly and potentially fatally, so to run up would not only be nigh-impossible physically, but also rather stupid. We walk.

The sun rises and bathes the mountains in light, the glasses are donned to prevent snow-blindness, and we walk slowly on and up. There is no-one about. Grouse-like birds whirr about us and choughs wheel high in the sky. We pant and wheeze on the steep uphill climbs, but the altitude affects us little as we have been high many times this trip so far and have drunk so much liquid that we pee every half-hour. Prevention rather than cure. We are both well aware of the symptoms and treatment of altitude sickness and once more employ the American adage of 'Listen to your body'.

The hours and the miles pass. At the third little stone shelter, we find a young Tibetan gentleman cooking up buckwheat bread with yak's cheese and omelettes. Both of us are ravenous and gobble down piles of the thick, round, stodgy bread and cheese before moving on. The man tells us that it is touch-and-go on the pass at this time. There is a lot of snow and therefore many people have turned back from this side. Our best bet, he says, is to go for a quick up-and-over, and pray that someone has come over from the other side early this morning and left tracks. 'Otherwise,' he goes on, 'you will need a guide so as you don't get lost.' He also wants to know where our boots and crampons are and do we have a tent in case a blizzard catches us half way up? Justin tries to explain what we are doing and once more we find ourselves caught up with someone telling us what we should or shouldn't be doing. We pay for the bread and leave.

From then on we encounter a number of trekkers, all heading up to the final stop before the pass, at Thorong Phedi. Here they will rest for a full day and night before attempting the final climb. We, however, will be going on and up today. These other trekkers are moving at a snail's pace, stopping every 150 feet or so to suck in lungfuls of the rarefied air. We are moving steadily for us, but we overhaul everybody, without exception. It is an indication of our fitness and makes us feel good.

Phedi is a tiny collection of three stone huts that sit on a ledge on the side of the hill. Everything everywhere is covered in snow. The relative safety of Manang is now a long way away and the guy who owns these huts knows it. He runs a small, dirty restaurant and charges astronomical prices. Apparently he is the boss of the Manang Hoteliers Association, which means that if you want to start up a hotel in the Manang area, you need his permission. Phedi is an ideal catchment spot for trekkers coming or going over the pass and therefore the best spot for a hotel. By chance, the chairman owns the only dwelling and for some reason no-one else has been allowed to build here. We sense a bit of foul play. Anyway, the guy has a monopoly, knows it, is making a large pile of rupees and will probably be able to retire to the sun in a year or so. Best of luck to him.

Justin and I shovel down noodles and copious cups of *chai*, get some information on the conditions from a Frenchman who came over from the other side early this morning, then set off. The time is half past eleven. We have already been going for six-and-a-half hours.

The next three hours were the hardest and most exhilarating of my life. Words can hardly describe the experience. The faint trail leads steeply up and over the snows and after half an hour we are a long way up and well out of sight of Phedi. We are quite alone. As we climb, the sheer immensity of this land fills me with wonder, but I can only look up briefly, for all my effort is going into climbing. My breath rasps in my throat and my legs start to feel dead. The altitude headache comes on as my brain starts to cry out for oxygen. There are too many false summits to count, the snow is deep and has softened in the morning sun and the wind blows hard and sharp in our faces. All around us are towering peaks, glaciers, snow cornices, ice seracs (pinnacles), endless snow-covered ridges, each one higher than the last and all of this under a brilliant blue sky. The sun beats mercilessly down on our heads but the wind whips away any heat it might have held and it is very cold. My moustache freezes to my face and my toes have already gone numb. Thank goodness for the double layer of material I had sewn into the front of my shorts back in Kathmandu.

Justin is going well. It's all I can do just to stay with him as he plods relentlessly up through this snow and ice wilderness. He loves the snow and the wild emptiness of the place and he's always happier up here than down in the trees.

Then, we take a wrong turning. The track has all but completely disappeared and we find ourselves hacking up a near-vertical ridge. At each step we are sinking in up to our thighs, Justin is breaking trail and is soon completely exhausted. The lactic acid builds up and up in the legs, the lungs gasp for air, we are both so terribly tired. Out comes the compass and we stop and think for a second. There is a loud crack and on an adjoining mountain, a huge avalanche plunges down the slope, leaving a cloud of freezing white smoke hanging in the air. The wind is still blowing hard in our faces and we have to shout to be heard.

'What do you think?' I yell in my partner's ear above the noise of the wind.

'We're too high too soon surely.'

'I agree! See the faint line in the snow on the side of the slope down there? That could be our path.'

'Or it could be just the path of some snow that's rolled down the slope.'

'Yes, could be, but what other choices are there?' My feet are rapidly turning to ice.

'Absolutely none!' Justin's face is set in a mask of discomfort and exhaustion but I can sense his determination to keep going.

'Right, let's go for it then.'

We stumble heavily back down the slope we have just spent nearly an hour climbing, then traverse a wide gully, and trudge up towards the line. It has to be the path, it has to be. I don't want to spend the night up here, nor do I want to go back down. We'll find the right way up to the pass, somehow.

We hit the line in the snow and it becomes obvious that this is indeed the way. We trudge over the top of this slope and into a maze of gullies and spurs. Where is the top? This climb has become a mass of false summits. I get a second burst of energy and break trail. Justin begins to suffer an altitude headache and the effort of breaking trail in the deep snow has taken all the energy from him. He settles in behind me and we climb as one. I look back occasionally and we exchange a thumbs-up sign. I am so exhausted that I can barely lift my arms to signal to him. The sides of my feet and my toes break the trail, but the snow is harder now we are higher and the effort goes more into staying on the side of the slope and not sliding off. Maybe crampons would have been a good idea after all. It blows harder. Then finally, after a lifetime of false summits, we reach the top and the rest of the world opens up before us.

I am so happy that I give Justin a hug and we stand there for a few moments, leaning into the freezing wind, gazing out at the rooftop of the world, totally in awe. I shall never forget that moment. We had made it over the gateway and our hundred-day target was still possible.

Evening saw us tired and sore but very happy, in a lodge at Muktinath, 5,100 feet down from the pass. We slept like dead men.

Chapter 13

KALI GANDAKI

We both woke feeling rather wretched and had a lazy breakfast. I couldn't eat much for my bowels were doing acrobatics and I had to rush off no less than four times. The tiredness in our bodies had asserted itself today but we reasoned that as we went lower, we should feel better. Last night we talked of spending a few hours here looking around, for the village is steeped in history.

Muktinath is a centre for pilgrims, both Hindu and Buddhist. There is a Buddhist Gompa here as well as a temple to the Hindu deity Vishnu. The area is special because of the natural gas jets that produce an eternal flame. This mix of earth, fire and water creates the mystique that surrounds Muktinath. Some of the pilgrims who come here have walked from as far away as the plains of India.

Also here is a micro-hydro facility set up by Intermediate Technology. The electricity is used for lighting and cooking and here too are the famous hot showers, with water heated by the excess electricity that would otherwise be wasted. A living, breathing example of how simple, applied technology can be made to work in the Third World.

I thought of our friends at I.T. back home and wondered if they were thinking of us at this time.

We set off down the hill, heading for the deepest valley in the world, the Kali Gandaki. This river valley cuts right through the Himalayas from north to south and passes between the massive bulks of Annapurna and Dhaulagiri. The drop from the summits of the mountains to the bed of the river is over 18,000 feet. Up here at Muktinath, the land is dry and arid and dead. It is a landscape of

Overleaf: The Kali Gandaki valley, the deepest valley in the world

windblown sand and tortured rock. Few trees can survive, for the monsoon does not reach this far up the valley, and only a few carefully tended fields produced high-altitude crops. The hillsides are coloured shades of striking yellows and browns and the colour scheme of yellow hills, white mountains and blue sky seems almost unreal, like a photograph that has been badly touched up.

We ran on and down. My bowels got the better of me again and twice I had to dash off into the scrub. One unfortunate young Tibetan lady got rather a shock when I bared my bottom not twenty feet from where she was collecting timber. There just was no time.

Jharkot – fortress town in west Nepal made of mud

Down through Jharkot, an ancient fortress town. *Kot* in Nepali means 'fortress' and we would come across many *kot* towns in the next couple of weeks. A man here is carrying thirty-foot-long plastic piping through the streets. He has to walk sideways to fit and his knees tremble under the weight. The long, black pipe bends at each end and will surely break. Herds of scrawny-looking donkeys and cattle are being herded through the angled, cobbled alleys and a tinkling of the bells, which hang around their necks, fills the air. The mud walls of the houses are crumbling with age and neglect and curious wrinkled faces peer out of half-shuttered windows, watching the world go by.

Jharkot – Ancient mud buildings falling into disrepair

Down in the valley, a cold, grey torrent twists a tortuous path through the gravel- and rock-strewn bed. The path follows the river bed itself and the running is easy enough. This is 'stubber' country though, so some concentration is needed. The sun is hot, my legs are tired and I think I'm suffering a little from dehydration. I tuck myself in behind Justin's plodding figure and we jog steadily down.

During the rest of the day we run south out of the barren northern Himalayas and into the tree-covered southern slopes, where firs breathe life into the soil and turn the world green. The villages seem cleaner, more organised, with paved alleyways, flat roofs piled neatly with wood for the stove, carved shutters and village taps that work. Only the dogs are as uncivilised and unfriendly as ever, snapping at our heels as we pass. This is the country of the Thakali people, well known for their trading skills in Nepal and Tibet. All the time the Kali Gandaki rushes by, gathering speed as it descends, and up above the fir-trees, Dhaulagiri and the Annapurnas look down on us all.

Justin is thoroughly enjoying himself and the two of us are getting along well. We laugh and joke and there is little or no tension between us. Times are good right now and he is full of enthusiasm for what we are doing, telling any trekker who wants to know and proudly relating the story of our progress so far. It is amazing to think that not eight months ago he was sailing a boat as a profession, hardly good training for this sort of expedition, and yet here he is now, running across the most mountainous terrain in the world, and even enjoying it. Disgraceful!

Day Thirty, and nothing can go wrong. Racing along, running up every slope the land can throw at us, legs pumping, sweat flying,

Human stone crushing machine in west Nepal

through three-sided tunnels high above the river, then down again and, panting, we soak our heads in cold streams. We are beginning to harden to the task. Stopping little, pushing on, keeping going. Western Nepal is only a day away, and there we will be away from the 'Pancake Trail' at last.

At the village of Tatopani, we sit and soak in the hot springs that bubble up from under the rock. The dirt oozes out of our bodies and our aching muscles are soothed by the piping hot water. But the water is too hot for us to soak for very long and we are put off by a Japanese man, who struts around in a black thong, embarrassing the local Nepalis as they wash their clothes at the springs.

From Tatopani, the trekker's trail heads south-east back towards Pokhara, while ours heads south-west down to Beni. On, on we run, both now beginning to feel tired and thirsty from the day's effort.

In the tiny, wooden and leaf-thatched village of Tiplyang we met Bhaktabir Pun, a retired Gurkha Captain. Now he is sixty-five years old and still wearing the khaki green coarse wool shirt of his army days. The cuffs are turned up evenly to the elbow and a crease pinches the sleeves. Old habits die hard. Bhaktabir joined illegally aged sixteen close to the start of the Second World War. He fought in Africa, Iran, Syria and Germany and was a prisoner of war in Italy for eleven months. After the war he spent time in Paris and London before travelling back to India by ship and hence to this village, his home. Now he has very little. A bare house, no electricity or running water, and a simple life of sitting and smoking his pipe, for he is too old now to till the fields or travel to trade. His bronzed, wrinkled face and crooked hands speak of years of experience and hard work. It is amazing to think that this old man fought in the same place as my grandfather during the Second World War.

Later, the track forked. I ran on down the low road and Justin took the high road. Mine was wrong, very wrong. After fifteen minutes of scrambling over loose scree and earth, I found myself balancing precariously over an old landslide about a hundred feet above the river, which roared hungrily below. I could see Justin high up the hill above me, tiptoeing gently over the treacherous ground, but on the right track at least. My track had disappeared altogether. With every step up, the loose rock and earth gave way under my scrabbling hands and feet and tumbled down into the river, leaving a small cloud of dust in the air. I could feel my heart

Bhaktabir Pun – Ex-Gurkha Captain

hammering against my ribcage. Looking up, I could see Justin waving and pointing off to my left. Was there danger? Is that a better way to climb up? I followed his direction and saw what he was pointing at. A young Nepali man was scrambling down the slope, barefoot and nimble, as he followed the side of the cliff down the edge of the landslide. He stopped a few feet above me and off to my left, his spindly little legs covered in dust and his face full of concern. He beckoned me over and I slowly edged across the sliding rock to join him. As I reached the tiny platform where he stood, he gave me a wide toothy grin and set off back up the way he had come. He was like a mountain goat, nipping up the near-vertical scree with ease, placing his feet on tiny juttings of rock and using his arms only to steady himself. I clawed my way up slowly behind him, sweating and cursing at my stupidity for getting caught out so badly.

Back in the tiny track, I sat and gasped lungfuls of air. The little man gave another grin and disappeared off on his way. It was a typical Nepali gesture. He had put himself at some risk in order to help a total stranger and he probably didn't even think twice about helping out. My respect and admiration for these people was increasing every day, and I wondered if I would have done the same thing for someone else in these circumstances.

Having sufficiently recovered, we ran on. The 'Himalayan Shuffle' took over and we moved into neutral. I started up a conversation about plans for the future when we were back in Britain and it went some way to taking our minds off our tired limbs and aching shoulders. Although the conversation was full of hope and positive thoughts, it belied the real state we were in. Both our faces and lips were peeling. Mine was only minor peeling but Justin's face was literally falling apart, the skin drying right out and coming off in lumps, leaving raw, pink and sensitive new skin underneath. My knee had begun to ache painfully again, Justin's ears hurt (we suspected *Otitis Media*), both our stomachs were churning away, we had diarrhoea and Justin's ankle was paining him again. How on earth we had made it this far was a mystery to me.

The last hour to the village of Beni found us split up again. I began to feel better and strode out, determined to get to our chosen goal for the night. As I saw it, if I was far enough ahead and just kept going past any lodges on the way then Justin, poorly as he was, would have to keep going. A little cruel perhaps, but we had to get on. Later on in the trip Justin would have to use the same tactic on me.

It was at times like this that we hated each other the most, but both of us were aware that it was helping the expedition to succeed. We would each be silently cursing the other for being too far in front, or too far behind, or for some thoughtless remark or deed and yet, in the grand scheme of things, these petty irritations didn't matter a jot. The only thing that mattered was getting to the finish and at the end of the day the pressures of the run were shelved for a few hours and we relaxed and laughed together again.

In Beni, a bustling little market village on two levels by the Kali Gandaki River, Justin's ears gave way completely. *Otitis Media* had struck in earnest and his head was filled with agonising pain as his infected eardrums throbbed mercilessly. This and his disintegrating face would be enough to make most people lie down and succumb to it all. But not Justin. He found out that there was a small hospital and a number of tiny pharmacy shops here at Beni, so he took himself off and returned an hour or so later with several small packets of pills wrapped in old newspaper. A course was started at once in an effort to knock the ear infection on the head as soon as possible. When he laid all the various pills out on the table, he looked like a travelling pharmacist himself and I couldn't help but burst out laughing at the sight. Justin glanced up from his pill-popping with a look of annoyance, then his face broke into as big a smile as he could manage in the circumstances and we laughed together. Suddenly life wasn't so bad after all.

Chapter 14

REMOTE WESTERN NEPAL

The following morning, after our first mosquito-ridden night since the Gorkha trail a week and a half ago, we decided on a late start. Ahead lay remote Western Nepal, where we expected food to be in short supply and the tracks to be small and largely unused. We were leaving the 'Pancake Trail' at last. No tourists, no lodges, no nothing.

In a tiny shack I had a full cut-throat-razor shave and a crew cut and Justin went to visit the little hospital. He had caught the *Otitis Media* in time and during the night the pills had done their job and beaten the infection. He bought a cheap baseball cap and angled the wide brim so that the sun was always kept off his raw and peeling face.

By eleven o'clock, looking rather dapper in new haircuts, we are heading west. Our target, Darbang, is just fifteen miles away. The track is easy and follows the Myagdi River upstream, and we are walking all day today in order to let ourselves heal a little. The river is wide and brown and noisy, the sun is hot and the people on the track are friendly. Poor old Justin is getting some funny looks from people when they see his black and red burned features. He jams the baseball cap firmly down on his head and soldiers on, obviously in some discomfort but uncomplaining.

We pass through another village called Tatopani (the name in Nepali means 'hot spring'). Here the smell of sulphur is very strong and our nostrils crinkle at the onslaught. In the valley everything is ripening: wheat, corn, onions, bananas, cabbages, potatoes, even a papaya tree. Butterflies, larger than I've ever seen, flutter about us

Ed in a Nepali home

on fluorescent black, blue and green wings; water buffalo graze lazily, their bottom jaws dripping thick white saliva as they chew the cud; two cows, yolked together, walk round and round the post to which they are tied, driving the stone wheel that grinds the corn; ladies in coloured skirts toss wheat into the air to separate the chaff; and some young boys wield ingenious, rattle-type devices to do the same thing. To these people the land is life. They work it and worship it and appreciate it for the life-giver it is. As I pass by on the track, I wonder what they would think of a frozen chicken, of the rows of flavoured yoghurts or of fish fingers and microwave chips in a supermarket. Surely it would seem so unreal to them, so totally divorced from their own simple, age-old ways of providing themselves with a living. Do they really need Western society and ideals; indeed do they really want them? My thoughts turn to the charity work we are involved with and to our friends at Intermediate Technology. Their approach is to work with the people of Nepal. Unlike so many other charities and government

Separating wheat from chaff in a Nepali village

A thatcher at work

aid bodies, I.T. do not dictate what the Nepals of the world should do, they just ask the question, 'How would you like us to help?' This must be the right way, for then Nepal takes its development into its own hands. Because it controls its own problems and solutions, it will take care to succeed in any projects it undertakes.

Looking around at the sights and sounds of this Middle Ages farming society, it seems obvious that change must come only in the most simple of ways and over a very long period of time. To do it any other way would not only fail but might even leave these people worse off than before.

I think of Leah, working hard to raise money for Intermediate Technology. She will still be walking on her trek to Everest Base

Camp, but soon she will be flying home to resume the fund-raising efforts. I remember the generosity of all those who gave money before we left; all those who showed such faith in us before we even started the run. I know that those people are rooting for us now as we stagger, sore and peeling, westwards towards our halfway point at the Nepalese border, only a couple of weeks away.

We walked slowly into Darbang in the early evening and looked around for somewhere to spend the night. The dusty track had given way to a neatly paved little path, which led through a street of stone- and mud-built homes. From one of the grander houses, a two-storey structure with green shutters and a new balcony on the first floor, stepped a short but very powerful-looking man of about forty-five. A paunch hung over his trouser belt and his large, nearly bald head gave him the flat, menacing look of a heavyweight wrestler. He was a slightly larger version of Bob Hoskins and every bit as frightening as the characters that man portrays in his films.

Tirthendra Gauchan, now known as Hoskins, was the area Panchayat chairman and greeted us with the type of grin that could turn a man to stone. In broken English, he welcomed us to his village and showed us upstairs to the two wooden beds that were ours for the night.

'You must pay whatever you think this is worth,' he said, as we shook hands, mine disappearing into his great meaty paw.

Hoskins obviously held great power here in Darbang. People moved about him with the studied care of those crossing a field having read the 'Beware of the Bull' sign on the gate. When he laughed, a great booming sound, even that was threatening, and everyone laughed with him. He was obviously the kingpin, yet he treated us with grace and much goodwill. A twinkle in his eye betrayed him as a gentler giant than he had at first appeared, and as he ordered that a goat should be killed for us, I could see he was thoroughly enjoying our presence. We protested feebly at the killing of the goat, but he said that it would soon be getting cut up anyway and that now was as good a time as any. Anyway, it was most unusual that any foreigners ventured out this way.

Outside in the courtyard, the condemned beast was brought bleating into the arena, a small, clear patch of paved ground to the side of Bob Hoskins' home. A small crowd of villagers had gathered and were watching the proceedings with the bored air of those who had seen the kill a hundred times before. Two men manhandled the goat to the ground, one sat on its hind legs and the other knelt on its shoulders and, grasping its horns, pulled its head back to expose the neck.

Hoskins sidled into the area. A large knife hung from his belt and he had donned shorts in preparation for the blood he was about to spill. He stood over his prey for a few seconds and looked at the surrounding crowd. The goat stared up at its executioner, its eyes wild and bulging and full of terror, a strangled bleating sound burst from its mouth and it struggled to free itself. The man holding its horns flexed his muscles and the goat could do nothing.

Hoskins' eyes found what they were looking for, which was us. He waved and grinned, then, pulling the knife from its sheath, he bent down and plunged it into the jugular of the beast. Blood spat hot and crimson from the gaping hole and the goat's legs kicked once, twice, then its eyes rolled upwards and it was dead. Hoskins was hacking at the neck, opening it right up; his feet were spattered with blood and he looked at the two men holding the goat and grinned. This was fun!

Within an hour the goat was unrecognisable for what it was. Hoskins, centre stage throughout, butchered the animal with a fluidity and expertise that I had never seen before. Nothing was wasted and that night we feasted on flesh, pancreas, liver, heart and kidney. Hoskins produced two bottles of beer and, in our dehydrated state, we were drunk within minutes. What a night it was.

The next morning saw two sore-headed Himalayan runners jogging out of the village and up towards the Jalja La, our last real pass in Nepal. The sun was hot early on and we stopped to drink from crystal streams. The rich meal last night caught up with us and several times one or other of us dashed off the track into the bushes to relieve the pressure in the bowels.

By midday we have climbed steadily high up the side of the valley. Justin is feeling a bit sick but is drinking lots of water and is still going. White-faced monkeys roll around on the ground playing, then see us coming and disappear into the trees, crashing through the undergrowth as they make their escape. The villages are few and far apart and very simple; and the people are friendly farming folk with smiling faces and impeccable manners.

We pass through villages named Dharapani, Takum, Sibang and there we sit drinking hot, sweet, black tea, watching the vultures wheel and soar far below. In Phalai Gaon we ask a small group of ladies, who look as though they are grandmother, mother and

Close to the border of western Nepal, you don't lie down in the sun for too long

daughter, for water. The young girl races off with a small red jug and I feel so guilty to have asked. How far she has to go, I don't know but she is gone fully fifteen minutes. She returns all smiles, and we drink and run on.

We make our way down to the river, the Dhora Khola, rushing crystal clear over its rocky bed. Waterfalls tumble down from all sides and trees and brush colour the slopes a rich green. On the way up again, with our legs aching already and feeling a little weak from hunger, we take the wrong path and find ourselves scrabbling up yet another rough slope to find the right way again. At a little wooden hut on the track, we come across a group of tired men travelling east. They give us some directions for the pass and we move on and up.

Ten minutes after we leave the hut, the sky suddenly clouds over and the world turns grey. The scent of rain fills the air and barely have we donned our waterproofs, when a violent wind lashes down the valley. We are in the lee of a small spur so don't feel the full force of this sudden wind, but the men sitting outside the hut get hit by surprise. Clouds of dust and natural debris are picked up and whirled around and we see two men literally blown over. One chap, trying to lift his loaded basket inside the hut, is blown off the side of the track, his loose, flowing clothes having been whipped up and wrapped around his face. Then, as quickly as it arrived, the wind dies then disappears, leaving blue sky and flattened wheat and barley fields.

At Lamjung we were still climbing and stopped to sit in a rickety little house with a group of elderly ladies, who 'oohed' and 'aahed' at my pictures of Leah and my family. They were such a happy bunch and laughed aloud all the time we were there. I found it infectious and laughed with them. We scoffed mountains of *daal baat* while another raging wind tore by outside, this time bringing rain with it. I dressed up to the eyeballs in my waterproof gear, ready to take on all nature could throw at me, and stepped outside. The rain promptly stopped, the sun came out and the ladies laughed even louder.

We left the laughing ladies of Lamjung and headed up to our pass. Soon the banana trees were far below and we were climbing through thick rhododendron forest, where mosses dripped off rotting branches and tiny birds were the only living things to be seen. As the views opened out below, a rainbow glinted wetly at our feet and the high peaks of the Himalayas were spread out before us once more.

Two hours later and well tired, we topped the Jalja La at 10,000 feet. It had been a real slog but we had done it in half the time everyone had said it would take. Over the top, the scenery changed dramatically for we were in high pasture country. The grass was short and tiny temporary stone shelters dotted the expanse of green. All around were jagged peaks of black rock and snow and to the north a magnificent white Himalayan giant towered above it all.

Our feet were cold and wet as we had come up above the snow line. Thankfully much of the snow had melted and now existed only in patches, but the wind was freezing and bit into our already painful peeling faces. We stopped and spent a few minutes stripping off and putting on extra layers of clothing in an effort to keep warm. The catch was that to put our thermals on, we had first to strip everything else off as thermals work best next to the skin. So there was always a moment when, naked to the elements, we got a lot colder, before getting warm again. We made the change in record time and ran down the gently sloping west side of the pass. It was four o'clock.

We had been going for eight hours already today, with just an hour off for rest stops, and were now pretty worn out. The *daal baat* had been a real blessing but ahead of us lay a long, empty and very remote valley.

A few hundred metres down from the pass, we found the source of the Uttar Ganga River as it trickled under the ice, and followed it down. We seemed to go on for hours. Every little rise left us gasping for air. Our legs had run out of energy for the day and we plodded on through the wilderness, one behind the other, both silent and suffering. I expected, but did not relish, a night out. We had no tent and, although our sleeping bags were meant to be waterproof, it would not be a welcome prospect to sleep out in this cold. I began to feel very lonely in this wilderness and was thankful for my partner's presence.

For two hours we jogged and walked and staggered down the valley. The two hours felt like twelve and as the tiny collection of stone shelters that was Gujer Ghat came into view, the feeling of relief was indescribable. A thin wisp of smoke drifted from the roof of one of the shelters and we knew that people must be at home. A number of horses were scattered over the green valley floor and a few well wrapped figures were rounding them up for the night. Gujer Ghat is a staging post for people coming or going over the pass. No-one lives here permanently and these little stone shelters are only just big enough to keep out the worst of the weather.

We arrived outside the shelter from which we had seen the drifting smoke and an old hag with wispy hair and several teeth missing welcomed us in. We must have looked very drawn and cold, for she made a great fuss of sitting us by the fire and keeping us warm. The hut was extremely simple, just an earth floor and a few logs for the fire. The old woman, warm enough in her striped head scarf, purple waistcoat, bright green waistband and long, loose-patterned skirt, stoked up the fire and the flames rose orange and red and warm. A string of white stones hung around her neck and got in her way every time she leaned over the fire. She was cooking on two long branches of wood, the ends of which were alight, and the cooking pots sat balanced on top. All around were her possessions, wrapped in dirty rags. The *daal baat* was on the boil. Smoke filled the room and we all squinted as it wafted into our eyes. Outside, the wind was rising, but in there, the fire crackled and spat and warmed and I was content.

Later on that night, I had to crawl out of my sleeping bag, leaving its delicious warmth, to have a pee. Outside in the dark, the air was cold and frosty and as I looked up, thousands of stars filled the heavens with a clarity that you only see when out in the wilderness. I remembered my walking expeditions in Scotland when, laying out my bivvie bag on a high hill, I would watch the stars appear one by one, marvelling at the space and beauty of the night. I stood and stared at the glittering heavens until the biting cold forced me back into the comforting warmth of the sleeping bag, and slept.

At five o'clock the tiny bleeping alarm in my watch sounded and I tried desperately to ignore it. Just another few minutes wouldn't hurt, surely. I heard Justin's alarm go off as well, a quiet rustling as he turned it off, and then the silence returned.

'Justin,' I murmured sleepily.

'Uuhhh!' unconscious.

'Are you awake?'

'Uuhhh!' semi-conscious.

'It's five o'clock.'

'Uuhhh!' conscious but despairing.

The silence returned and my nose, the only bit of my body exposed to the air, told me that outside my lovely warm bag it was freezing. I really did not want to get up. We both lay there, hanging on to sleep and putting off the inevitable for as long as we dared. 'It's bloody cold out there.' Justin was fully conscious at last.

'We've got two choices,' I said. 'We can either lie here all day in a wonderfully comfortable pocket of warmth, or we can get up and expose ourselves to the freezing cold and attempt to run another twenty-five miles over the most demanding country in the world.'

'Oh, I'd far rather do the latter,' said Justin with theatrical sarcasm.

'I was afraid you'd say that.'

'After three then. One, two, three.'

We launched ourselves out of the bags and packed up in a record time of seven minutes. A quick stretch and we were away.

As we descend this valley, the huts slowly become more numerous and more people appear. These scattered communities are terribly backward and poor and consist of widely spread, single storey, stone buildings, not unlike the shelter we slept in last night. The people are very Tibetan in appearance. They dress in rough cloth and wear open sandals woven from plant fibres. How they keep warm in this weather beats me. The countryside is wide and alpine, trees cloak the slopes, and green meadows flank the icy torrent that now thunders down the bottom of the valley.

By nine o'clock we have reached Dhorpatan, a remote and barren-looking slope on which are huddled grey stone shelters. On the edge of the village is the reason why Dhorpatan is on the map at all. The King's hunting lodge.

Every now and then King Birendra Shaha flies out here into the remote western part of his kingdom, to relax at his lodge and do a spot of hunting of mountain goat and panther. He lands at the tiny, rough airstrip below the village and walks up to his bit of paradise in amongst all this poverty.

Justin and I run past the entrance to the lodge. It is empty and the national flags flap lazily in the chill breeze. A small, carefully kept path of white chippings winds from one building to another and an incongruous little yellow sign in English points the way to the toilets. Incongruous because it seems so ridiculous to find this little haven of luxury way out here in this poorest of lands.

In the village, a middle-aged man in blue trousers with a yellow stripe down the leg cooks us up some *daal baat* and potatoes. The sun has warmed up the valley and we sit outside the smoky hut trying to get some directions from the small crowd that has gathered. Our maps are of little use, for there are no names on them that the locals can recognise. Either that or my pronunciation is rotten. Probably a bit of both.

The food revives us a little but both of us are tired and weary and aching. My left knee hurts and I have developed a hacking cough that makes my throat painfully dry. Justin's face is slowly improving but he too is developing the niggling injuries that seem to plague us these days. For the first time I begin to worry about the damage I may be doing to myself in the long term. This is my second running expedition and I'm wondering if my body is beginning to tell me something.

Running puts immense pressures on muscles and joints. It is estimated that, as you run and land on one foot at a time, four times your body weight is taken on that one foot. The shock is absorbed by the muscles and joints of the ankle, the knee and the hip. Justin and I are also carrying eleven pounds of kit, giving a combined weight of 716 pounds on one foot for approximately 30,000 steps per foot per day. That's a lot of pressure.

Life now is full of annoying injuries. If it's not the ankle it's the knee, or the shin, or the thigh, or the calf, etc . . . I don't think our injuries ever get any better; it's just that we seem to get used to them. But even that does not stop the worry of possible permanent damage. Still, I knew all this before I set out on this trip, and the main goal remains as irresistible as ever. I have to strive to get to the end, despite any injuries, despite what the future may hold. To finish is everything.

Later on in the day, we get lost. The tiny community of Nisheldhar has eluded us for hours and now, when we should be there, we find ourselves down by the river, wondering why on earth we set out on this crazy venture in the first place.

As we climb up out of the river valley, the village at last suddenly appears. The buildings are so low and merge into the surrounding scenery so well that it is no wonder we missed it. A small group of excited-looking, weather-beaten men point us back down to the river for the path to Khore. We go cursing and swearing back down the hill we have just climbed.

I was always the more vociferous one at these times. I hated getting lost or 'temporarily mislaid' as we called it. It usually happened through our lack of concentration or inability to glean all the relevant information from people about the route. Getting lost was a waste of time and a waste of energy and it made me feel stupid and therefore angry. After a bit of ranting and raving to myself and the world in general I always felt better. Justin, on the other hand, would say very little and just keep it all to himself. But I probably did enough ranting and raving for the two of us anyway.

A long, mainly uphill slog through the late afternoon followed. We ran and stumbled through thick pine forests, clinging to the steep slopes, and emerged high up on the north side of the valley, in the community of Tatung. An old man with wrinkled, sunken cheeks showed us into his house and we sat on straw matting and ate potatoes with the rest of the family. Chickens were running about all over the place and one of the daughters 'shooed' them from one corner to another. This family of nine – father, mother, four girls and three boys – are living a bare existence, yet they welcome us in with open arms and share their food with us without a thought. Their natural grace and generosity touches my heart. I show them my pictures of my wife and my family which instantly brings on the homesickness and I lay my head back against the mud wall of the house and think of Leah and my friends and of roast beef and Yorkshire pudding.

Slowly but surely we traversed western Nepal. The hours grew into days and in my mind the running, the land and the people merged into one massive blob of effort. We were crossing the grain of the land, passing through valleys and over ridges and aiming for our most westerly point in the hills of Nepal, Dailekh, just six days away.

There were three major hill villages on the way: Rukumkot, Musikot and Jajarkot. All were ancient fortresses and sat high up on the ridge-tops several thousand feet up from the river. Before each was a long, hard climb up well trodden paths, then a crazed dash on painful legs down the other side. Every ridge brought a new view, a different experience, and in our minds we ticked them off as one might tick goods off a shopping list. The hills stretched away to the horizon, shimmering blue and grey, and in hidden valleys, blue rivers roared over boulder-strewn beds.

The land became more green as we moved west, and on the sides of the slopes, people of the Magar and Bho Tiya had carved terraces and were growing rice, corn and wheat. Water buffalo grunted in their efforts while pulling the plough, and tiny birds with bright yellow, red and black plumage flitted about the banana trees and bamboo groves. The houses were two-storey mud-built structures, coloured white and orange and thatched on top. Curiously they were the same design as those of eastern Nepal.

On the trails we met porters carrying enormous loads, wedding processions, people travelling to their fields, and teachers on holiday visiting their home villages. On one lonely track just down from a ridge-top, we stopped where a thin trickle of water slithered over a moss-covered rock and butterflies darted from flower to flower. Here too was a group of middle-aged men, squatting by the side of the track. They each held an ancient flintlock rifle and were off into the hills to shoot mountain goat and deer. What a cheery bunch they were and, sitting there chatting away in pidgin English/Nepali, I would have loved to have gone with them. What adventures they must have.

At Musikot we sat in a grotty little tea hut and watched the vultures soaring on their nine-foot wingspans. Justin had somehow found two bottles of beer, which was a wonderful alternative to the usual chlorinated water, and within minutes we were pissed again. What a wonderful feeling it was, after the excruciating, sweat-soaked effort of the morning, to sit in the shade of the tea hut and feel nicely tiddly and light-headed. The beer helped us to laugh and it took away some of the painful realities of our chosen lifestyle. Back home I do not usually drink and so one beer in my dehydrated state was lethal. What fun!

On, on we ran, the miles disappearing underfoot. Our socks were wearing out and we both had large holes where our toes poked through. Justin's had also torn at the heel and I'm sure the Nepalis wondered why we wore them at all. When we had bought the socks from Thorlo back in England, we had been told that we could

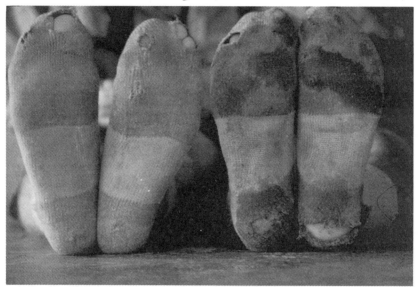

The second pair of socks each start to suffer

run a marathon with just the socks and no shoes and they would not wear through. We had taken the company at its word and had proceeded to run just under a marathon (with shoes) every day for the last thirty-six days. This was the second pair and they were bloody good. Our sum total of blisters so far this trip had been just four. Admittedly our feet had been well hardened before the run started in earnest, but four blisters in thirty-six days is pretty good going.

The kit then was holding out fine but our bodies were now approaching their limit of endurance. My diary from Day Thirty-seven describes how I was feeling at the time:

I went into automatic pilot and noticed very little as the endless dirt tracks and ups and downs rolled by. Where the track flattened or went down we ran, but otherwise we walked. It was all we could do just to keep going at all.

I'm feeling tired all the time now. I've been going for thirty-seven days over the most mountainous terrain in the world, so it's no wonder really. The bounce has seemingly gone from my legs. When I run, it is with a great deal of effort both up and down. The annoying thing is that, when walking, we get to places so slowly, and that can be demoralising. When we run the miles fly by and the villages appear in quicker succession. The feeling of achievement is thus accentuated.

I go through stages during the day. At the beginning I usually feel tired and even after stretching, very stiff. Then after an hour or so of going I start to loosen up and feel good, all muscles work and the miles fly by. Then at about eleven o'clock, I get very tired. The lactic acid build-up in the legs is so very quick and can leave me breathless even after a few steps uphill. When it clears I'm OK and I settle into the plod. The rest of the day becomes an endurance test. A lot of positive thinking keeps me going until five or six o'clock, when we finally stop. I think, because I'm so tired, that some of the fun has gone. The trip is now a real challenge to mind, body and spirit. It is about endurance, patience and perseverance. It's a pity about the 'fun' bit though.

One night we were holed up in someone's home and a small group of travellers arrived. Nepali men heading east for Rukumkot and caught out by the nightfall: it gets dark very quickly out here. One of their number had a small tranny radio and we tuned in to the Nepali news. This news program is read first in English, then in Nepali. The newscaster's voice rang out from amidst the crackles of interference: 'The King has dissolved the Panchayat system, the Prime Minister has resigned and democratic principles have now been adopted in Nepal.'

We listened, wide-eyed, a handful of *daal baat* stopped dead, only halfway to the mouth. What amazing news! The Panchayat system dissolved, democracy, freedom of speech; an amazing change. The people of Kathmandu and other cities had been fighting for months to change the system. Many innocents had been killed in violent clashes between police and demonstrators over the past few weeks and now those demonstrators had their wish: a democratic Nepal. It really was amazing news. Such astonishing and fundamental change and in such a relatively short period of time. We whooped with joy at the newscaster's statement that the King would now allow other political parties to exist and that a full inquiry into the abuse of human rights by the security forces was to take place immediately. We waited in anticipation for the newscaster to read the same news again in Nepali. These people in the hut with us would go wild.

But as the incredible news was repeated in their home language, it caused not the slightest commotion. The travellers continued to shovel *daal baat* into their mouths and no-one expressed any emotion at all about the happenings in the capital. Indeed the only people who seemed in the slightest bit interested were Justin and myself.

We put the lack of excitement on the part of these people down to the fact that out here in western Nepal things had changed little in the last fifty years. The fact that Nepal was now a democracy and not a benign dictatorship would affect them not a jot. This was a movement led by the new intelligentsia of Nepal, by the students in colleges and universities in the major towns and cities. To the hill peasants, it meant nothing, so why get worked up?

Added to this was the fact that the King of Nepal is the spiritual head of a Hindu state and is worshipped almost as a god by the simple folk of the hills. Therefore he can do little wrong and eyes and minds are simply turned away whenever the many and varied rumours of corruption and extortion rear their ugly heads.

Here we were, Justin and I, in a country in the midst of revolutionary change, and yet no-one seemed to give a damn.

We reached Dailekh on Day Thirty-eight and bloody satisfying it was too. Our special permits from the Nepali Immigration Service allowed us to move only as far north-west as this point. From here we would have to cut south-west down onto the Terai plains to run one hundred miles up to the dodgy border crossing at Mahendranagar.

Dailekh, the most westerly point in the hills of Nepal, had been a target for us for days. The little hilltop village bustled with life: hundreds of people bought and sold and haggled and threw stones at the dogs that padded around in the dirt. It was a filthy but busy little place and we found ourselves a bed, a thin, worn out, bed-bug-ridden old mattress on the floor, in a dusty room.

We bought four bottles of the wonderful 'Iceberg' Nepali beer, toasted each other wearily and drank. Within minutes the world was fun again.

'What a couple of alcoholics we're becoming,' said Justin with a grin that showed he didn't really care. He took another long

Justin in a Nepali home awaiting arrival of *daal baat*

swallow, his Adam's apple working overtime.

'I'm not half as thunk as you drink I am,' I slurred. The room was already moving slightly and Justin kept on splitting into two.

'You're drunk,' said Justin.

'If you think I'm under the alcofluence of incohol you're very much mistaken,' I prompted him, or rather, both of him.

We were both giggling stupidly, sprawled back against the splintered wall of the room, clutching our precious bottles of beer.

I looked across at my partner. God, what a state he was in; and I must have looked the same. Face sweat-streaked, hair matted and dishevelled, a disgusting-looking t-shirt and the whole covered in the dust and dirt of the trail. He looked knackered.

'You look knackered,' I told him.

'And, as Winston Churchill said to Lady Astor, you look ugly, but in the morning I shall be sober.'

We took another pull on our beers and chuckled softly. It was good to be laughing together again. The past few days had seen some tension between us. The going had been hard and dry and there had been little food compared to central Nepal. The sheer effort required every day was getting to both of us and it was becoming harder and harder to control our feelings. Arguments were always sharp and biting but thankfully short-lived and, well, we were still together, weren't we? I sat and looked with half-closed eyes at my partner slumped against the other wall and wondered if we'd still be friends at the end.

'To travel hopefully is a better thing than to
arrive, and the true success is in the labour.'
Robert Louis Stevenson

Chapter 15

THERE'S TIGERS
IN THE TREES

The plains were just a day and a half away and surely it would be downhill most of the way. We jumped the gun again and built our hopes up on an easy time ahead to the border. But we could not have been more wrong.

Out of Dailekh I was running too close behind Justin as we skipped over the broken, rocky track. Half-asleep, I hit the 'stubber', stumbled, then my world turned upside down and I flew through the air and crashed down on the rocks. My head, arms and elbows broke my fall. My first thought was for my legs. A broken arm I can run with, a broken leg I cannot. I lay there, sprawled over the rock, shocked and groaning in pain. Justin helped me up. My arms were dead, my ego was bruised but otherwise I seemed to be OK. Determined not to let my fall get me down or undermine my confidence I immediately set off running again, my torn and bleeding arms throbbing painfully. God, what a stupid berk I was. I hate making silly mistakes and I swore at myself for not concentrating. Just one little lapse of concentration on these treacherous slopes and 'bang' a broken leg and goodbye expedition. This was the first time one of us had fallen so far. I must have been getting tired to the core.

Justin hated it when I got into one of my angry moods and always went very quiet while I ranted and raved the annoyance out of my system.

At the next water stop, I bathed my wounds in the healing liquid and thanked Justin for picking me up. We ran on together again.

Our target was Surkhet, a town at the end of a dirt road that ran north from the Terai into the hills. Because of the road, Surkhet is a place where the hill people of western Nepal come to buy and sell goods. We met many travellers on the well trodden track. Some had been walking for ten days just to get a few necessaries, otherwise unavailable in the hills. We jogged through tiny communities of tea shacks, where people sat and drank tea or ate chapatis. Those heading south had baskets of farm produce to barter in the town, while those heading north had done their bartering and carried back metal pots, paper and cloth. We passed one young, barefoot lad carrying a sick old man on his back. He had fashioned a sling around a basket and had tied the old man to it. He now carried the whole, massively heavy and awkward bundle with a strap around his head. The pressure on his joints must have been incredible yet he seemed to make good enough progress. He was acting as ambulance, taking the sick man, his friend's father, down to the hospital at Surkhet, and had been going for three days. Herds of goats, each with its own tiny backpack, thronged the track. The kids panic as they come face to face with us, do a little turn, jump up and down off all four legs then rush off to find mum, bleating loudly. The shepherd always brings up the rear with his fit and rather wild-looking dogs, which I studiously avoid.

After twenty-two miles, 3,000 feet of climbing and 4,000 feet of descent, we reached the town and spotted our first vehicle in sixteen days. A rickety old orange truck caked in dust, it was an indication of what was to come. We scoffed mountains of *daal baat* and *momos* cooked up for us by the lady of the lodge in which we were staying, washed our filthy clothes and sewed up a few holes that had begun to appear in the seats of our trousers.

In an effort to keep going as far west as possible we decided to take a chance and look for a little-known track that would lead us west onto the main east-west Nepal road. The alternative to this track was to run for perhaps two days south-east down the road from Surkhet, then cut back west again once we hit the main road. This track, if we could find it, could save us two or three days.

We crossed the valley to Plate, then climbed up and over a small hill and ran down to Rani *ghat* (bridge) over the Bheri River. This was the same river we had followed way back between the *kots* of western Nepal. Here we drank chlorinated water and tea and ate glucose biscuits. The people here were very poor and the wizened old man who served us tea looked underfed and hassled by his bossy wife. The whole area was covered with trees and their fallen leaves crackled underfoot. It was hot and the earth was dry and dusty.

Over the bridge, the track splits continuously, then virtually disappears. We have no map, just a scrappy bit of paper with a couple of scribbled names of remote villages, and we are desper-

Ed, keeping clean . . . ish

ately hoping to meet someone to show us the way. It's a terribly
lonely and depressing feeling, stuck there in remotest Nepal, with
no track, no views because of the trees and absolutely no idea
whether or not you are heading in the right direction. We are now
climbing up a white, boulder-strewn, dry river bed. The huge steps
we have to make are exhausting and the sweat pours off us and
drips onto the rocks. Every now and then we climb the banks and
thrash around in the bushes trying to find the path but to no avail.

'What's that up ahead?' says Justin. He is standing on one of the
banks, waist-high in undergrowth, and staring up river. I follow his
gaze but can see nothing.

'What can you see?' I ask.

'People; people up ahead. Come on, let's catch them.'

We pound up through the boulders with the distinct feeling that
someone is looking after us today and catch up with the people
Justin has seen.

A small wiry man in long shorts, a little boy and three girls. They

look up with alarm as we arrive, panting and grinning stupidly. We were just so damned pleased to see them, indeed to see anyone. The three girls, all teenagers, were dressed up as if they were going to a party. They were wearing white skirts and scarlet red tops and their long black hair was tied back and topped with red bows that completed the pretty picture. The man had a withered arm, which sat awkwardly inside his shirt, and the little boy sported a shy smile. They were going our way and we decided to stay with them until the track improved. The girls giggled away as we took a picture of us all with the self-timer. They were a wonderful splash of colour in the hot, dry land through which we were passing.

Two hours later and a couple of thousand feet up on a high ridge, a man with a huge, bristling sergeant major's moustache boils up some tea in a pot. In the house with us is a travelling doctor who is waiting for the locals to arrive for their immunisation jabs. As we sit and watch the flies crawling over any exposed part of our skin, a few ladies appear at the doorway with their babies in their arms.

The doctor barks at his two young helpers and they go outside to set up surgery in the shade of a broad tree. He opens up his box of sterile syringes and serum and proceeds to immunise the children against such nasties as diphtheria, whooping cough, tetanus and tuberculosis. The child would suckle at its mother's breast while the doctor shoved in needles galore. More mothers and children arrive and soon the little area under the tree is full of trusting women, some of whom will have walked many miles to get here. The doctor and his assistants move amongst the mini-throng with calm efficiency.

The drugs in the box are donated to Nepal by UNICEF and the country is in the middle of a national immunisation programme. At present only fifty-four per cent of the young are inoculated against killer diseases and the target is to have eighty per cent inoculated by the end of the 1990s.

We are both terribly impressed by the professionalism of the whole scene. The whole operation underlines the extra difficulties that exist in mountain areas for we are a long way from the road. Yet the advance communication party has obviously done a good job in getting people to come to the right place at the right time.

A couple of hours of descent and we are suddenly on flat ground, deep inside a forest. Our view is minimal: a sea of trees on all sides and patches of blue sky above. Jungle sounds pierce the silence as monkeys thrash about in the high branches; the odd bird calls the alarm at our approach; and termite mounds abound – castles of mud piled eight foot high by thousands of the tiny beasts.

I feel hemmed in, with no real view, and only the sun to tell us in which direction we are heading. It is a totally new feeling; not unpleasant as such, just different.

We run for what feels like hours, shuffling on one behind the other, taking it in turns to lead. Two wooden huts appear and we have stumbled on Danwatal, a tiny army survival training camp. Only two soldiers are here; the other eight are out in the forest somewhere. They give us water and warn us to beware of wild animals in the trees.

'What animals are there?' we ask.

'There are tigers in the trees, and elephants too,' they reply. 'Do not go into the forest at night. It is very dangerous.'

It isn't far off night-time now. We thank them and run on through our tunnel in the trees, not altogether sure if they were pulling our legs or not, but unwilling to take the chance. Suddenly the trees fall away and there in front of us is the road. A wide, dusty, raised track, cutting directly across our front, this is the east-west highway of Nepal, our route to the border at last.

On the map, the road is marked as a main, paved highway. On the ground it is a pitted, dusty, pot-holed, endless brown snake that stretches across the Terai for as far as the eye can see, cutting a swathe through the dry jungle on either side.

We clamber up, stand and look both ways. Nothing. Not a hut, a vehicle, or a human being in sight. Nothing. Each way stretches to oblivion. This truly is the road to nowhere.

100 degrees and it shows

For three days we run and sweat in the hottest temperatures of the trip so far. It must be a hundred degrees, perhaps hotter. The highway, or rather, the dirt track destroys vehicles and their rusting and broken skeletons litter the sides. Trucks sit with wheels removed and laid flat, now propping up smashed suspension, or leaning crazily sideways, stuck in yet another rut.

But it is the dust that affects us the most. It coats the surface of the track six inches thick and we kick up a cloud of it as we run. It sucks at our feet, disguises hidden rocks and leaves us choking. It gets into our eyes and mouths and fills our shoes.

On all sides the dense, dry forest stretches away into the distance and our views are limited to the front or the back. To step off the track would be to find ourselves lumbering around in the brush, lost within minutes and vulnerable to the bestial dangers within.

But there is life too. Every hour or so, a battered truck or bus lumbers slowly by, bouncing from rut to rut and leaving us coughing on huge clouds of dust. The people inside probably don't even see us.

We see grouse and colourful turquoise jaybirds, yellow wagtails and a kingfisher. Egrets flap on lazy, white-washed wings as we approach and the occasional vulture soars high above.

Within an hour of starting in the morning we are both absolutely filthy. Our clothes are caked in dust and our bodies are grimy with muck and sweat. Whenever possible we dunk our t-shirts in water and put them on wet in an effort to cool down. It is so hot that the wind is like a hair dryer and the wet t-shirts are dry within minutes.

Evenings find us ensconced in tiny wayside huts, sleeping on wooden boards and sweating in our down sleeping bags, not daring to come out for fear of being eaten alive by the mosquitoes that plague us.

Then, on Day Forty-three, we reach the border town of Mahendranagar and run the last four miles to the border post itself as Banbassa. We have made it. Halfway at last, and a forty-two day crossing of the most mountainous country on earth behind us. We wonder whether we could claim some record. 1,000 miles have passed underfoot and we've only got the same to do again. The prospect is just too appalling for words so we put it to the back of our minds and concentrate on trying to get through the border into India.

This border post has been closed to all foreigners since 1987, due to India demonstrating against a political decision by the Nepalese government to accept certain arms deals with the Chinese. It was the Indians then who were the aggressors. They had shut off all but three border posts between India and Nepal and thus starved the Nepalis of much-needed materials like kerosene and metals.

However, I had two hard-won letters to show to the border guards, one from the Indian government and the other from the Nepalese Immigration Service. But still I had that awful sick feeling in the pit of my stomach as I knew I had to deal with petty officialdom again. We cleaned up at a water pump, donned our rather clean-looking Reebok tops and, looking reasonably respectable, strode up to the guards, permission papers at the ready.

On the Nepalese side, a young policeman glanced at our papers and waved us away. 'No-one allowed through here,' he said.

'Oh God, it's started,' I thought to myself.

I explained quietly that we had special permission and asked to see his superior. A fat man in a white shirt arrived. He had a smiling face and I breathed again.

'You must show this to the Chief of Police,' he told us. 'There will be no problem.'

I smiled insolently at the young policeman and we walked off to find the Chief of Police. We found him sprawled outside his headquarters in the sun having a nap. As we approached, one of the policemen standing guard at the gate turned and muttered something to him. He sprang up, smiled a toothy smile at us and bade us sit down. He read the letter and told us that we could go through. Much stamping of passports followed and away we went, first stage successfully completed. Now, the Indian border.

We walked through no-man's land, full of hope and clutching our Indian permission papers. Then the fun started.

As we arrived at the small jumble of wooden huts that was the border post we witnessed a man being severely beaten with a stick for dropping some medical supplies. We were sat down in the porch of one of the huts in two tiny, low chairs. Three comfortable, bored-looking officials, two with very brown teeth and corrupt smiles, sat facing us from behind a desk. The whimpers of the bleeding man who had just been beaten carried up to us on the breeze. I got the feeling that this was not going to be quite so easy.

I showed the papers, passports, visa extensions and special permit given to us by the Home Ministry. The three of them sat there and proceeded to pick holes in all of it. First it was the Tipp-Ex on the letter. (I'd warned the Ministry in Delhi about that but had been told everything would be fine); then the dates on the letter (we were here ahead of the time stated on the document); then the fact that they had not received a duplicate copy from the Ministry.

I explained, protested, pleaded, bargained, suggested and threatened, but to little or no avail. These petty little dictators just weren't interested in letting us through. They had all the power they needed to let us cross over, but no, they couldn't possibly make a decision based on their own initiative; that would be asking too much. The fact that they had not received a duplicate copy was not our fault, nor was the Tipp-Ex. The dates, maybe, but then they were based on wild estimates of time and distance before we'd even started running. It just seemed that they were determined not to let us through from the start. The two brown-tooths were as smarmy as could be and were playing with their power. I was boiling with anger inside.

Eventually, after one-and-a-half hours of heated discussion, we came to an agreement. One of the officials, a brown-tooth, would go to Nanital where he would telephone Delhi to get our letter confirmed. Nanital was the nearest place with a telephone link to the capital and it was sixty miles away. The round trip might take two to three days and we would just have to wait.

'Go back to Nepal and come back here at nine o'clock on 26 April and if my friend (the brown-tooth) has got permission then we will let you go through. However if he cannot make the call, if the lines are down or something, then you will not be allowed to pass. Is that clear?'

'Oh yes, quite clear,' I seethed.

We took the long walk back through no-man's land and into Nepal. Both of us were very depressed and for me, two years of planning and preparation now hinged on one telephone call. I tried to be philosophical about the whole thing, but failed. In China, in 1988, my partner and I had dealt with enough petty officialdom to last a lifetime. Here in the Himalayas, we had done everything possible to enable us to pass through the border, yet still petty officials stood in the way. The expedition was crumbling before my eyes. I could see the headlines back home, 'Himalayan run abandoned at halfway point', or 'Runners forced to quit after just forty-three days'. Life could not have been worse.

Back in Mahendranagar, we took stock of the situation and made alternative plans. Our options were threefold. We could fly or bus it back to the permitted border crossing 350-odd miles to the east, pass into India then bus it back round to the Indian side of the western border. That would mean a round trip of 700 miles and perhaps four days in order to cross just a few feet of ground. Another option was to wait here and see what happened in two days' time, and a third was to try and contact our friend Miss Gulati at the Indian Home Ministry in Delhi to get her to sort it all out.

All we really wanted to do was sleep but instead we leapt on a

A typical 'Pancake Trail' inn

Stretching aching muscles – A twice daily ritual

Far Left Above:
The alternative river crossing –
a wheeled trolley on 2 cables
Below:
Justin in a village in Uttar Pradesh
Left:
The local ambulance, with patient
Below:
The 'Border Roads Organisation' sign
Overleaf:
A precarious resting place

Overleaf:
Justin, contemplating ending it all
in the Barai Nala river
Far Left:
Kashmiri man
Left:
Dynamite used for blasting paths
into the cliffs, left out in the sun
Below:
Kashmiri man smoking a water pipe

bus and endured a bone-jarring, four-hour ride south-east to a town on the plains called Dunghari. Here, there was a telephone line into India and the following morning I managed to place a call to Miss Gulati. I explained the situation and she promised to do what she could to help. I put the 'phone down, wondering how on earth she could sort it out in such a short time. We decided to rely on her, leapt back on the bus and bounced and crashed our way back to the border, hoping for the best.

Nine o'clock the following day, Day Forty-five of the trip, found us sitting in the same nervous position. Our three officials arrived, old brown-tooth having only just returned from Nanital. We were to be allowed through.

A great wave of relief swept over me. We had done it. The first foreigners to pass through in three years, and now our hundred-day target was possible. We had wasted two days and were wound up something rotten, but in the end all the preparation had borne fruit. We just sat and grinned. Miss Gulati had done her bit, somehow.

We then sat and endured four hours of the most bungling, inefficient and laughable bureaucracy that I have ever seen, as our passport and travel details were taken down and duplicated a hundred times. But by three o'clock we were in India at last.

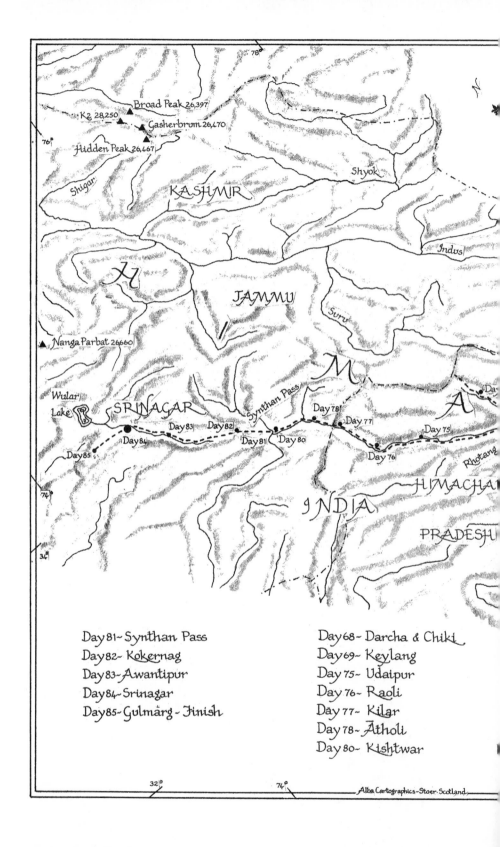

Day 81~ Synthan Pass
Day 82~ Kokernag
Day 83~ Awantipur
Day 84~ Srinagar
Day 85~ Gulmärg - Finish

Day 68~ Darcha & Chiki
Day 69~ Keylang
Day 75~ Udaipur
Day 76~ Raoli
Day 77~ Kilar
Day 78~ Atholi
Day 80~ Kishtwar

Alba Cartographics·Stoer·Scotland.

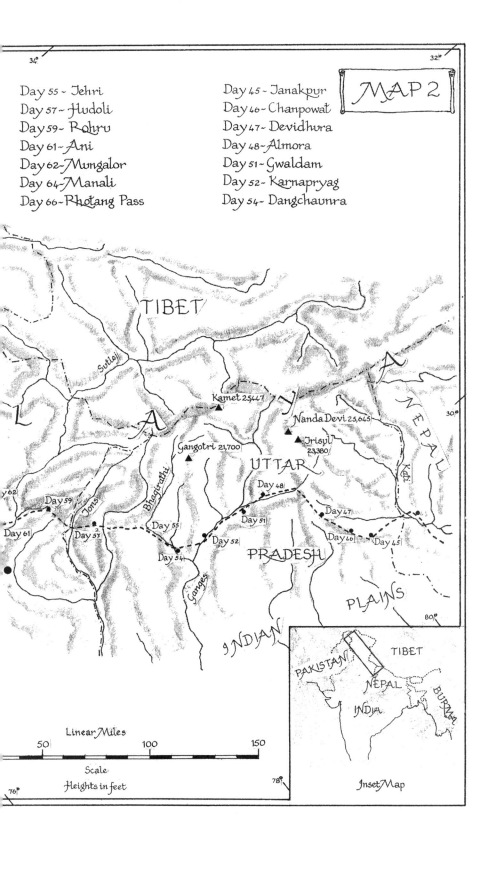

Day 55 ~ Tehri
Day 57 ~ Hudoli
Day 59 ~ Rohru
Day 61 ~ Ani
Day 62 ~ Mungalor
Day 64 ~ Manali
Day 66 ~ Rhotang Pass

Day 45 ~ Janakpur
Day 46 ~ Chanpowat
Day 47 ~ Devidhura
Day 48 ~ Almora
Day 51 ~ Gwaldam
Day 52 ~ Karnapryag
Day 54 ~ Dangchaunra

MAP 2

TIBET

Sutlej

Kamet 25447

Nanda Devi 25,645

Gangotri 21,700

Trisul 23,380

UTTAR

Day 62

Day 59

Jons

Day 61

Day 57

Bhagirathi

Day 55

Day 54

Day 52

Day 48

Day 51

Day 47

Day 46

Day 45

Kali

NEPAL

PRADESH

Ganges

INDIAN

PLAINS

Linear Miles

50   100   150

Scale

Heights in feet

PAKISTAN

TIBET

NEPAL

INDIA

BURMA

Inset Map

Chapter 16

A SLAP IN THE FACE

We arrive in India and the twentieth century immediately slaps us in the face. Metalled roads, cars, fancy buildings, well dressed people, electric light, fridges and cold drinks. What a change!

Just a few miles away, people in western Nepal are living in mud huts and cooking on wood fires. Here radios blare, overhead fans cool the rooms and kerosene fuels the stoves. *Daal baat* is replaced by a number of small, spicy dishes and people mostly eat with spoons rather than with their hands.

We have entered the province of Uttar Pradesh, a vast area of land housing 300 million people. Popularly known as 'the multitude', the vast majority of these people live south of the hills in the plains, and yet here in Tanakpur, just inside the border, we feel swallowed up by a bustling, yelling mish-mash of Indian society.

This region, like the whole swathe of the Indian Himalayas, is steeped in history. It is important to Hindus and Buddhists alike as the Ganges, the holy river of the Hindus, runs right through the centre and at Sarnath, Buddha first preached about the 'middle way'. Over the centuries, it has been ruled by successive powers. First the Buddhists under the Empire of Ashoka 2,000 years ago; then the Moghuls and, as their rule declined in the late 1700s, the Gorkhas of Nepal expanded their borders further and further west to take in this land.

It was the British who finally put a halt to the Gorkha expansion by 1815 and secured the area as its own north-west frontier. By the time of independence in 1947 the region had become known as Uttar Pradesh and it remains so-named today.

India – A Hindu holy man in Uttar Pradesh

The northern part of this province houses one of the better-known of the Indian mountains, Nanda Devi. Not one of our 26,000-foot peaks, as it tops out at 25,405 feet, but an impressive giant all the same. Here are the dwellings of the Hindu gods and therefore the whole region is dotted with sacred shrines and temples. Hindu pilgrims have travelled to these parts for centuries and continue to do so today, walking vast distances, visiting a variety of holy places and living off people's good will. We were to come across many of them in the next few weeks.

The other marked change, having entered India, was the people's appearance and manner. They were taller and their faces were long and gaunt. We had first noticed this change in Nepal as we approached the border, but it had been the style of dress that we had picked up on. The women wore long, brightly coloured *saris* that elongated their figures and gave them an air of some sophistication; while the men dressed either in the trousers and wing-collar shirts of the seventies or in loose, flowing robes. Their manner was rough and uncaring and, dare I say it, twentieth century. It was quite a change from the quiet, gentle manner of people in Nepal.

India was a very different place indeed and, after the simplicity of life in western Nepal, Justin and I felt rather shell-shocked by it all. The eight-mile run in the heat into Tanakpur left us both with more than a touch of heat stroke and we lay on the beds in our hotel, relishing the cool breeze supplied by the overhead fans and getting bitten to blazes by a plague of mosquitoes.

'This is the most comfortable place we've stayed since Kathmandu,' murmured Justin.

'And with a more intelligent type of mosquito as well.' I slapped another one of the buzzing little pests and it spattered on my arm, spilling my own blood from its gut. 'Three more days or so and we should be in Almora.'

'That's my little test, isn't it,' said Justin.

'What do you mean?'

'Well, you've done your bit, getting us through the two borders, and now I've got to do mine. The kit.'

'Of course, yes. New shoes and socks. That's going to be bliss.' I looked down at the very sorry and worn-out looking pair of Reeboks. They had carried me all the way from Kathmandu, over all types of terrain and now they were knackered. 'Bloody good shoes those, but I'm looking forward to a new pair.'

'If they're there,' said Justin.

'They'll be there.'

'Well, I hope so. I've got this horrible vision of the hotel manager, to whom I sent the kit, walking around in a brand new pair of Reeboks and telling us that the bag was stolen.'

'I guess we'll just have to wait and see then, won't we?'

'I guess so. Can you imagine what a new pair of socks would feel like?'

'Oh God, don't. I've had enough excitement for one day.'

We drifted off to sleep and dreamed of fluffy, clean, fresh-smelling new socks.

The following morning we ran north out of town and started to climb. We had to regain all the height we had lost by coming down onto the plains. Down here the heat was close and oppressive but up ahead in the hills, the clouds were gathering and a low rumbling of distant thunder heralded the approach of a storm. When we got to the tiny tea shack at Bastia, the heavens opened and our dry world turned suddenly into a torrent. The rain crashed down and threatened to carry us away, hut and all. With us, sheltering in the gloom, was a Buddhist monk and a Hindu family. Had we been carried away we would have been a little ark housing a microcosm of Indian society. I put the thought to the Hindu gentleman but he did not know what I meant by the 'ark' and looked at me as if I was quite crazy, so I let it drop.

The rain ceased and the sky cleared. A delicious smell of wet vegetation filled the air and we ran on and up. This mountain road switched back like crazy and so, on spotting a tiny, leaf-covered track leading up through the tree-covered slopes, we followed it, hoping that it will cut out some of the distance. It did, and we resolved to use these tracks whenever we could find them in the future.

In India, much of the track and footpath lies unused and unknown, for people travel by road these days. This manifested itself most clearly whenever we asked for advice on the route.

'Follow the road,' we would be told. 'It's much easier.'

'It may be easier but it's also much longer,' we would mutter in reply. What might be fifteen or twenty miles away on the road could be cut down to as little as three to ten miles by taking all the shortcuts. Our estimates of the distance of the trip had been made mostly on straight line measurements, so any shortcut on these roads was most welcome.

In trying to get the local people to give us some clue as to where these shortcuts were, we would draw a map in the soil. It was a simple dollar sign, the 'S' shape being the road and the vertical line being the possible track. We must have drawn this map in the soil of north-west India a thousand times. Sometimes we got a result, sometimes we did not. But 'shortcut' became such an attractive word to us that Justin decided that if he ever had a dog he would call it 'Shortcut' in memory of this time.

From the wooden shacks of Chalthi, where we wolfed down chapatis spread with banana and sprinkled with sugar, we took the best shortcut of the day. Climbing high off the road above the Ladhna River we followed the old trade route, now disused but still a substantial path. As we strode out, feeling good about being up in the hills again, the Indian Himalayas spread out around us, and blue ridges and green valleys became more visible the higher we climbed. Small communities of mountain people dotted the slopes, with huts and houses perched on every available flat. Most of the homes are made of brick and concrete; and there is electricity, the pylons marching up and down the steep slopes, bringing civilisation into the hills. Some households even sport solar panels. Old men and women sat outside smoking or washing clothes or just chatting, and barefoot children stood and stared as we ran by. We stopped occasionally to refill the water bottle at a water pump and to check that we were going the right way. Here, we were able to ask men and women. This is a change from Nepal, where generally the women would hide away and we would only be able to speak with the men. But here the ladies, young and old, looked us straight in the eye and had no hesitation in helping us out.

Late in the day we are back on the road again and running into the town of Chanpowat. We have run for thirty-three miles today and the legs have had enough. The town is a colourful sprawl of red, blue, yellow and white houses over the low hills, and in the centre, the market bustles with activity. A marriage ceremony whistles and bangs down the main street. Trumpets blare tunelessly and a man is bashing a drum and a cymbal. Two grinning, made-up male dancers prance around swinging carved swords and tiny round shields. The swords flash in the evening sunlight and, as the two men weave around each other it's a miracle that neither gets struck. In the surrounding crowd, everyone is smiling and clapping; everyone, that is, except the groom. He is sitting on a horse, dressed in scarlet shirt and green trousers, and looks miserable. Justin and I saw a couple of Hindu weddings in Delhi back in February and there too the groom looked as if the world was about to come to an end. In India it is the done thing to look morose and hard-done-by before your wedding, as you are leaving your parents and their household for the first time.

We mingled with the crowd and laughed and clapped with them. I asked one of a group of young men, a lad in his twenties called Harpal, whether this was an arranged marriage.

'No, no,' he shouted above the din, 'this is a love marriage.'

'Is that usual?' I shouted back.

'Yes, very usual. Sometimes the boy and girl, they fall in love and go to their parents for permission. Like these two people.'

'And what if their parents do not consent?'

'I don't understand.'

'What if parents do not give permission?'

'Well, no marriage.'

'That must be very difficult.'

He thought for a moment at this and said, 'But it is our way, our tradition.'

'Are you married?' I asked him.

'No, but my parents have found somebody for me, so maybe I will marry soon.' He laughed long and heartily at this prospect, then asked me, 'And what of you, do you marry?'

'Yes, I am. For nearly two years now.'

'And was your marriage arranged by your parents?'

'No, it was a love marriage, like this one.'

'Oh, you are very lucky. But where is your wife now?'

'Well, she is in England, very far away.'

'And you are on holiday on your own with your friend,' he stated.

'Yes, we are. A holiday of a sort.'

The weaving dancers with their twirling swords were dancing themselves into a frenzy and others in the crowd began to join in as the music crescendoed. We said 'cheerio' to our new friend and left him and the happy crowd to their revelling, so we could find somewhere to sleep the night.

The following morning we set off into a gathering storm. Dark grey clouds rumbled and lightning flashed in sheets and forks across the heavens. Then it threw it down. Buttoned up to the eyeballs in our thermals and Gore-Tex rain suits, we put our heads down and 'shuffled' on, the violent wind buffeting us from side to side and the

Landslide in Himachal Pradesh (India)

rain doing its best to find an opening in our water-proof layer. It was cold and miserable but at least we were on the way home.

Having passed the halfway point two days ago, I now feel very much as if I'm on the way to the finish. Absurd really, as there is still just under 1,000 miles to go, but it's the crossing of the halfway mark that does it. Justin feels much the same way and he is very much more animated these days. He laughs and jokes more easily and is thoroughly enjoying the daily feeling of achievement. This feeling is even more enhanced now we are on the second half of the trip and Justin is always grabbing the map to check on our progress to date. His mind wanders far ahead into the future and he talks of where we will be in two or three weeks' time. I, on the other hand, keep my feelings about finishing to myself and prefer to look just a few days ahead at the most. Because of the sheer physical and

mental effort required each day, I find that if I try and plan too far ahead then I only get depressed; but if I set short-term goals, the feeling that we are getting somewhere is accentuated and I'm much happier.

Later, the rain eased and the clouds were rolled back by a blue sky. The rest of the day passed in a blur of ups and downs, of pine forests and small, run-down villages.

Once, on a lonely mountain road, we were offered cannabis or some other intoxication by a group of village men. They beckoned to us insistently and made smoking signs with their hands and mouths. We declined just as insistently.

'But why you say no?' questioned one of the men, holding my arm and trying to stop me from going on. 'Every English like smoking.'

'Well, not these two, pal,' I retorted, pulling myself free from his clutches.

Up here in the hills of Uttar Pradesh, Westerners have come for years to buy dope and spend a few weeks sitting in some remote village smoking themselves to oblivion. The area is well known for it. The druggies and hippies are still in evidence and apparently the English are well known buyers. Most of the activity centres around Almora, the hilltop town just one-and-a-half days away and the location of one of our kit drop-offs.

The end of the day saw us climbing to the ridge-top village of Devidhura, a dirty scattering of shops selling bottles, bags, pots, biscuits and cloth. The laid-back villagers sit in their shop-fronts drinking tea or chatting with friends. An old generator thumps away somewhere and some men are weighing huge sacks of grain on a cumbersome set of pendulum scales. There is no guest house here, so we sleep in the forestry house, a smart white building with green shutters and doors. The views from here are stupendous for the whole Uttar Pradesh Himalaya is spread out before us.

I was in bed by half past six, having eaten nothing due to a dicky stomach. Outside a fabulous electric storm raged and was made even more powerful by the strange yellow evening light and our elevated position on the ridge. An enormous grey and black front of billowing, threatening cloud came racing towards us from the north-west. Lightning lit up the edges of the black menace and thunder shattered the clouds. The rain was flung down with such force that it bounced off the ground and the wind lashed the drops sideways creating a solid curtain of water. The sheer scale and violence of the storm was exciting and awe-inspiring and, back in the forestry house, I pulled the drawstring of my sleeping bag up tight and slept.

By the end of the following day we had reached Almora, an ancient hill station straddling both sides of a ridge. The tiny paved streets thronged with people and shops sold everything one could possibly need for daily use. This was our next staging post and we planned to rest here for a day in order to mend kit, have a good feed and write letters home. Justin disappeared off into the maze of alleyways to find the man to whom he had sent one of our kit bags. He returned two hours later triumphant. His hours of patient organisation in Delhi back in February had paid off and we had new shoes and socks at last. Sheer bliss!

We changed money, posted a parcel of excess kit back to our

friend Adrian Stones at the British Embassy in Delhi, wrote letters and postcards and ate fried eggs on bread, a wonderful change from the everyday diet of rice and spicy vegetables.

Then, for me, Almora blurred into a haze of stomach cramps and toilets. I thought I had a touch of dysentery. Up five times during the night, squatting over the hole-in-the-floor toilet, passing pure liquid, feeling sick and sweating buckets, I was not having a good time. So much for the rest stop.

By sunrise on Day Fifty I was feeling weak and thoroughly dehydrated. I had hardly slept a wink and my body felt very heavy and cumbersome. I knew I had to get out of Almora fast before depression set in.

A local chemist gave me some pills to swallow three times a day, which turned my pee a disturbing shade of orange; then we set off out of town. I am a firm believer in helping the body to cure itself by thinking and acting positively to an illness, but right now I just felt like a worn-out husk of a human being. Justin, by contrast, was feeling good and his cheeriness made me perk up a little. He told me of the hippies he'd seen in the bank when he went to change some money. A small group of long-term European residents of the area, dressed in what they must have thought were ethnic clothes, they were trying to get money moved from their homes in Europe to here. None of them looked as if they'd washed in weeks and they stank something rotten. The bank officials treated them with some disdain and it must be very difficult for the Indian people not to form their opinions of Europeans from these types.

Off the ridge and into the valley, we follow the Kosi River upstream. The river is green and meanders slowly through the mixture of pine and cactus and banana trees. We watch tiny kiddies leaping into still, green pools, shiny brown bodies and shouts of glee. Ladies thin and elegant in their brightly coloured *saris* walk gracefully by, balancing baskets and bags on their heads. Birdsong fills the air, crested tits, woodpeckers and flycatchers flit from pine to pine, and a beautiful tiny white bird with long, flowing tail feathers flees from its perch as we approach.

We stop at a village called Manan and find ourselves a room above a tea house to sleep in. The owner's elder brother arrives to greet us. Dressed in a smart, brown safari suit, he is the headman of the local area and, in conversation, gives us some interesting facts about the village, one being its 'ration card system.' After five years of living in the village, one becomes eligible for a ration card, and thus has access to the government-subsidised food that is brought up from the plains. All interesting stuff.

That night we slept undisturbed for ten hours and by morning my stomach cramps had settled and I had some of my energy back.

The day is warm and bright and we jog upriver, enjoying the bouncy feel of the new Reebok shoes. Over the Kausani ridge and down again, we are crossing the grain of the land and chance a footpath that leads down off the road to the north. We are running all the way, our feet skimming the surface, fresh with exhilaration at our speed. I have to dash off into the bushes a couple of times but otherwise I'm feeling fine. Donkeys weave drunkenly from one side of the track to the other; a stubborn cow is being ferociously beaten by its harassed and sweating owner; barefoot Indian ladies waddle along carrying huge loads; herds of goats are urged on by high-pitched whistles from the herdsmen and, down by the river, a small group of young women are washing themselves. They look up at us with smiling beautiful faces, oblivious to their semi-nakedness. We increase our speed with a sudden rush of adrenalin.

Then we are climbing again, 2,500 feet up to Gwaldam village, our target for the day. Our legs grow weary and the air becomes comfortably cool. Our ascent delays the sunset so that the golden ball seems to hang motionless in the sky while we climb. Then, as we reach the village and find somewhere to stay, the sun finally dips over the horizon and envelops us in the shroud of night. We have made twenty-seven miles today – not bad for a man with the world falling out of his bottom.

The days began to pass in a blur of movement. The sights and sounds of the Indian Himalayas unfolded to us as we traversed further and further west and slowly began to realise our dream. Each day brought its experiences and we settled into the Indian way of life. Always a part of the landscape, yet because of the nature of our expedition, always slightly remote. We questioned whether we were really experiencing Indian culture or whether, by always moving through, we were only getting a glimpse. We felt very much at home here now; things were less strange, and we relaxed. Our experience of almost three months' travelling through the remote Nepalese and Indian Himalayas, of staying with people in their homes and of travelling most of the time far from any beaten track was giving us a broad yet unusually intimate insight into a different way of life. We felt touched by the values and morals practised by these people, and although here we would always be foreigners, maybe we could adopt some of the admirable qualities of the people of the Himalayas when back home in Britain.

Yes, of course we were just getting a glimpse. Three months in a country of the size and social complexity of India can only give you that. But our glimpse seemed intimate and deeply felt to us and we both knew that we would carry the experience with us forever.

Day Fifty-two: we ran for thirty-nine miles today to the town of Karnaprayag, the greatest distance in any one day of the whole journey. But it was mostly downhill and on a road that twisted and turned downriver, numbing our minds with boredom.

In the early morning, I performed my now patented and well known tumbling stunt and went arse-over-tit on the dirt track. As usual, I was too close behind Justin and half-asleep in the dawn. No harm done except for a bruised ego.

On, on we run, with a wonderful, rhythmic forward motion. We are covering the ground at seven-and-a-half miles per hour, legs in neutral and minds wandering. Life seems to revolve around the road. It provides communications for the people of the hills, a chance to travel in hours to places which, before the road, would have been several days' walk away. It offers them the chance to sell their goods to a wider market and to buy the odd luxury. Electricity brings power and the lines branch off up the steep slopes to hidden villages in the hills. We pass threshing machines and turbines going full tilt. At a place called Thrali, on the bridge, we chat to Mr Singh Negi, who is surveying the flow-rate of water in the river at several points between here and Karnapayag. His measurements will be used to decide the position of the next hydro-electric project for this area.

Above and all around us the Indian Himalayas grow higher and higher but there is no snow as yet. Below us, the river has turned an ugly grey and it roars through its gorge with a noise that bounces off the cliffs and echoes in our ears.

Day Fifty-three is a shorter day, and we only cover twenty-three miles. Our limbs are tired and our muscles stiff. Legs are devoid of power, all energy having been spent on yesterday's effort, and both of us are yawning continually.

But the day brings its own fresh sights and smells. We pass five tall, gangly-looking men with walking sticks ambling along. They are dressed in very simple, orange-and-white cloth, their faces covered in dishevelled and uncombed hair and, walking barefoot, they carry tiny cloth packs slung over one shoulder. These are

Hindu pilgrims. They have shrugged off all the constraints of their past, maybe even leaving wives and children in the process, and have devoted their lives to worship. They are well respected by the people in these remote areas and manage to live off handouts from people along the route. These five men look terribly thin and scrawny and their lives, which are full of deprivation and hunger, must be terribly hard.

Justin helps an Indian family across the torrent

A hundred yards down the road we stopped at a tea shop. The five strange travellers soon arrived and squatted down outside the hut. We bought them a cup of tea each and one of them struck up a conversation via another man in the hut, who knew a little English. The pilgrim held up his stick for us to see. It wasn't a stick at all but a trident, a symbol of one of the Hindu deities. He and his colleagues were making a pilgrimage to a number of sacred pilgrim

centres and Hindu temples as part of their worship. He told us of the three main Hindu deities – Vishnu the Preserver, Brahma the creator, and Shiva the destroyer – and that Hindus are free to worship each in whatever way they see fit. The single overriding aspect of their religion is their belief in rebirth. The caste system which helps to stabilise Indian society is used in such a way that each individual will aspire to lead a life devoid of sin, thereby gaining membership of a higher caste in the next life.

Trident-man had long, shaggy black hair that hung to his neck and was tied with a piece of red cloth so it did not fall over his eyes. Through the gap in his grey beard a mouth, devoid of teeth, smiled gently at us. He had a serenity about him that calmed those in his presence. We both felt some affinity with these men, for in our own way we too were on a pilgrimage, testing mind and body; and we too travelled everywhere by foot.

Day Fifty-four: the road, the endless, boring road is tougher going than we had anticipated. The hard, even surface brings on repetitive injuries of the knees and ankles and it is only by doing constant stretching both morning and evening that we prevent our muscles from seizing up altogether.

Early in the day, we managed to get something to eat at a little stall. A man was cooking up onions and bits of fish in batter. I hadn't had fish since leaving England back in February. What a treat! I bought a few pieces from the man and was about to sink my teeth into the biggest bit when, just in time, I noticed an eye peering out of the batter at me. I had been about to crunch right into the head . . .urgh! Justin saw this and decided against trying a piece for himself. But the other bits were delicious, if rather bony, and would have been even better with a plateful of chips as well.

The food here in India is still playing havoc with our bowels. We have diarrhoea almost constantly, which only adds to the wearing-down effect on our bodies and, although we clean ourselves and our clothes as often as we can, ours is a pretty filthy existence. Back home we would have been shunned from society by now as being trampish and unclean, but here there are no prejudices and people take us in to eat or sleep without comment.

Day Fifty-five. 'Thumb up bum and mind in neutral'. My sergeant major in the Royal Marines had described the mental state we were now in very well. The miles rolled mechanically by and after twenty-five miles we reached Tehri, a dirty, ramshackle, noisy town in a narrow valley on the Bhagirathi River. The Indians here were pushy, surly and unfriendly and we spent two frustrating hours trying to find somewhere to sleep. But although Tehri is a rough, ugly town, it is also famous or, more accurately, infamous, thanks to the enormous Tehri dam project.

The dam, presently under construction, will be the biggest dam in the world when completed. It is a project funded by the Russians and the electricity will supply the cities in the plains with power.

But the dam will also create an enormous reservoir that will drown not only the town of Tehri itself but also all the land for twenty-five to thirty miles up the valley. 100,000 people will be displaced with just a token pay-off to cushion their loss, and the ecological balance of the whole area will be changed forever.

The Indian newspapers report that due to constant landslides filling up the valley, the amount of power that the dam will be able to produce will be substantially below the original estimates. The life expectancy of the dam has shrunk from 160 years to just thirty, and the cost of construction has risen by at least fifty per cent. According to the newspapers, nobody wants the dam except the politicians and the engineers and yet slowly but surely it rises from the valley floor.

One disillusioned young Tehri citizen pointed up the hill to the temple about 500 feet above our heads.

'That temple,' he said with incredulity creeping into his voice, 'will be covered with water one day, and so will all of this.' He spread his arms pointing out the surrounding town buildings. 'We'll be drowned forever.'

He indicated a small group of squat, grey buildings 1,500 feet up on the side of the valley. 'That is where the Russians live. They will be the only ones left.'

We spent an uncomfortable, bed-bug-ridden night in this condemned town and I wondered if it would still be here if and when I next came back to India in years to come.

Day Fifty-six: two hours out of Tehri and we have left its dirt and grime far behind. The views of green ridges and roaring rivers are now very ordinary to us and our sights are set on the small white kilometre posts and we jog along ticking up the distance. We run with our now characteristic shuffling gait which keeps us going forward at twice walking speed and allows us to keep running for long periods without stopping.

Our pace has very much evened out now, as we expected it would, but still I like to be in front. When we run side by side I cannot help myself feeling competitive and I increase the pace continually in order to take the lead. It's crazy after all this time together, but this competitive streak in me just keeps pushing me on. It's hard to explain and even harder to control. I've always been the one in front so far and now, as we even out, I start to find myself behind occasionally and I don't like it. I'm always looking for an opening in order to retake the lead and forge ahead again. I don't mention my feelings to Justin as there's little point. It's just the way I am.

Justin, on the other hand, is as steady and plodding as ever. He seems happy to be in front, side-by-side, or behind. It just does not seem to bother him. He is patient and kind and seems oblivious to the frantic motor instinct of his partner. Thank goodness we are so different, though, for I am sure that the two styles complement each other.

The road is endless, twisting round countless spurs and valleys where streams tumble down into the main river. Sometimes, to go just a hundred yards downriver, we have to run a mile in and out of an adjoining valley so as to avoid cliffs or dangerously steep scree slopes. By the time we reach Brahankhal we have run thirty-eight miles and I am as tired as I have ever been.

Day Fifty-seven. The road becomes a track, then a path, leading up through thick pine forest, where needles carpet the soil a soft red-brown. Himalayan starlings, sparrows and a kestrel appear through the trees. A buzzard perches, uncaring, under the nest of two thoroughly agitated magpies, and high above the vultures soar on enormous wingspans, keen eyes sweeping the ground for carrion.

From the village of Barkot we are climbing again, off the road and into some remote hills. We have no maps of this section and have scribbled a few names of villages down on a piece of paper and hope for the best.

The path is long and steep and rocky and a hot sun beats down on the backs of our necks as we haul our bodies upwards. Justin is burning again on his arms and legs and he spreads some white blocking cream over the offending parts. The villages on our route are backward, but the folk are warm and kind to us. Once again the difference between simple village folk and people living on the road hits home. The villagers are collecting hay at this time and their porches are full of bundles of the bright yellow brush. Mud and wooden houses are topped with slate. Some of the slate plates are as large as four feet square and must have required some effort to carry home from wherever they were quarried. The wooden houses have ornate carvings on their shutters and on the uprights of the porches. I can see flowers and leaves and other patterns, and the grain of the wood has been used cleverly in their design.

People are working hard, collecting hay, separating wheat from chaff and grinding corn. Everyone has a job to do. Only the old men with white beards and wrinkled, bronzed skin do nothing but sit and suck on their pipes. When we appear, all work stops for a moment as, wide-eyed, men, women and children stare at the two strange, sweating Englishmen. Often someone will give us water and amusement abounds as we fumble with the tiny chlorine tablets to purify the liquid for drinking.

Although the travelling is hard and the tracks are badly kept, although we lose our way a couple of times and spend two frustrating half-hours gaining lost height, we are sorry to come away from these remote places and back down onto the mountain road at Hudoli, our target for the evening.

Day Fifty-eight: what an awful night last night. We tossed and turned on the hard floorboards of the verandah outside a small hut in Hudoli. For some reason I could not stop sweating and the mosquitoes plagued me all night. My face felt bitten to bits and I managed to whack myself on the head a few times when trying to swat a mosquito that kept dive-bombing my ears. I'm sure I woke up more tired than I was when I went to bed.

All in all, it was not a cheerful Ed who set off across the Himalayas this morning. I was happy enough to 'shuffle' along without talking, just programmed on automatic. Justin's chit-chat got to me today and I was probably rather short with him a few times. I guess we all have our bad days. The trip has become rather an endurance event for me now. The days roll together and my enthusiasm for the culture has waned slightly. I feel keen to get to Manali and be out of Uttar Pradesh. There's been no real 'aim' in this state, no major town or mountain or temple to aim for. I like to have an objective. From Manali there are plenty. Three passes, the Zanskar range and of course the finish. But for now, it's a daily slog to get as far as we can. I knuckle down but sometimes it's hard to be cheery.

Justin is also tired, but he seems to be enjoying it more than me at the moment. He has become much more voluble and chatters away continually. I'm just being damn selfish and miserable and will have to snap out of it. I'd far rather have the current cheery Justin as my partner than the past moody one.

We gambled on a shortcut today, off the road and over a high ridge. By road the route to the village of Khunigar was thirty miles and we hoped to halve that distance, then run on to the river junction town of Tiuni.

The country was rough, rocky, high, thickly forested and beautiful. Just off the road at the old part of Purola, we stopped for what was to be the only grub for the next seven-and-a-half hours; a few glucose biscuits with condensed milk on top and a cup of tea. The tea came in real china cups, which always make it taste so much better.

From here, the trail – or trails, for there were many – led us up small rivers and streams and into the forest of pines. We passed a group of soldiers giving firearms instruction to some young men. The targets, painted on sacking, were fixed on the other side of the stream and the fire was directed by blasts on a whistle, all in a disciplined military fashion.

The next two hours took us way, way up and over the top of a faraway ridge. As we plodded up, feet crunching dead leaves and pine-needles underfoot, our muscles grew more and more tired. I sweated from every pore in my body. Why are my legs so useless now? It seems such an extraordinary effort just to put one foot in front of another. As we climbed, we entered a maze of wonderful, tree-drenched ridges. The slopes were all near-vertical and there seemed no way that men could pass through this massive, forbidding country. But pass through we did.

The track forked too many times for us to count. It meant taking a gamble calculated with compass and consensus. Generally we chose the route that led uphill, because if we had got lost it would have been easier to lose height than to gain it.

At one crucial fork in the track, two men were resting and having a smoke before heading up to Ringali on the ridge-top. They were going our way.

We were obviously being looked after by somebody today, for this opportune meeting was one of three that occurred during the day. We would go for hours without seeing a soul, then at the crucial time, a traveller would appear, our hearts would lift and we'd get the direction we needed.

Over the ridge at last, we paused for a while in a leafy glade where a dribble of water ran over a leaf and spattered quietly on the damp earth. We sat and drank and munched on the remaining glucose biscuits. The crickets and cicadas buzzed noisily in the surrounding rhododendron trees and the odd wood pigeon or turtle dove flapped between the branches. The cloudless, blue sky was criss-crossed by the black branches and twigs of the trees and, looking up, we found shapes of animals and faces in this natural jigsaw.

For two hours we ran and slithered down through the pines to the clear, cold river far down in the maze of valleys under the ridge. Wandering through idyllic, shady green clearings, where it would be a wonderfully relaxing experience to pitch a tent and sit and read for a week, I vowed to bring Leah back here some day. It really was a beautiful, peaceful place.

The end of the day sees us ten miles from Khunigar in the town of Tiuni on the Dhons river. The river dominates the scene. It is massively powerful and its thundering noise is ever-present. We have eaten well on rice and spicy vegetables and have found a dirty but comfy little room in a guest house for just fifty pence for the night. Tomorrow we will head into the province of Himachal Pradesh and on towards Manali, our next kit pick-up point.

Day Fifty-nine: I feel happier today, even though I've got plenty of excuses for being miserable. My legs have somehow recovered some of their energy and I am running well but this morning I had the raging trots. I don't know if there's anything worse in the world than running along a precipitous Himalayan mountain road with a painful, distended bowel but nowhere to hide. Only just in time did the bushes on the upside of the road appear and I dashed in to squat miserably, wondering if I'd ever be well again.

Later on, in one tiny shack, I noticed an old man, with his grey hair tied neatly on top of his head, squatting on the floor clutching what looked like a bundle of animal skins. On closer inspection, the animal skin proved to be the cover for a fascinating book. The skin was antelope and the book was written in a local language, native to only a few people in the Shimla district of Himachal Pradesh. The old man had learned the language from his forbears and he too would pass it on to the younger generations. Some of the book was given over to telling the future through palmistry. Once I'd got the old man's confidence, and had taken off my shoes and socks, I squatted by him and was allowed to handle the book. Its pages were browned with age and waxed to help preserve the print. With our pidgin Hindi we could only ask so much but it would have been fascinating to know more about this much-revered gentleman and his ancient book. Before leaving I asked him if he could predict how many children I will have. He grabbed my right hand, twisted my thumb into my palm, paused for a moment staring at the lines on the side of my hand and said, 'Three. Two boys and one girl.'

'The thing is,' asked Justin, 'are you going to let Leah know this?'

'I think I'll reserve judgement on that for now,' I answered. 'I guess I'd better start earning some money though, just in case.'

Ten miles and another four mad dashes for the bushes later, we were supping more tea and eating chapatis dipped in spicy vegetables.

With much banging of drums and blowing of trumpets, a holy procession came clashing past the door. A large crowd of people carrying an ornate, glittering, silver box on a stretcher at shoulder level arrived. The box was draped with a fine white cloth and to the cloth were pinned Indian rupee-notes. The men bashing the drums and blowing wavering notes from four-foot-high curved trumpets created no tune as such, just a noise. These people were carrying the box, which housed a tiny statue of one of the Hindu gods, to a temple fifteen miles from here. On the way, local villagers would come out of their homes and stick money to the white cloth. In return they received a blessing from the priest and got to touch the holy relic. The money would be used for the upkeep of the temple buildings. They moved on and a few men from our tea hut joined the procession too.

Justin and I ran separately today. I think it has done us both some good to spend time away from each other, so as not to impinge on the other's thoughts. We've been living closely together for a long time now and both of us need time on our own sometimes. It means that occasionally I am a long way ahead or a long way behind, depending on my mood for the day and my physical well-being. At this stage of the trip, though, it is mostly Justin who is in front. I manage to suppress my competitive instinct for a while and put my mind to planning the future. Our fitness and physical condition have evened right out now and at the moment he is going better than I am. It's bound to happen, really, and I am trying hard to be realistic about it. But the motor instinct inside me smarts whenever I find myself struggling, and it's a real mental effort to relax and not try to race to catch up and overtake. The racing way only leads to exhaustion and we've got a long way to go. I'm tired, I've got a very sore and runny bottom and I'm going as fast as I can.

Day Sixty. From last night's stop at Rohru we ran for twenty-five miles and, despite continuing bowel problems, I seem to have my energy back and was running strongly once more. The sun shone out of a blue sky dashed with cotton-wool clouds and the air was wonderfully cool.

From Machoti, the dirt road gave way to track and we climbed up the side of a sun-splashed ridge to the village of Bachunch. There, we stumbled across an old temple and spent half an hour prodding around in overgrown courtyards, peering in at the stone and wooden carvings of the gods. Eight-foot-high stone obelisks, intricately decorated with carvings, housed the effigies, and a red-and-pink ribbon had been draped over one of them. The grass grew up through the gaps in the paving stones and a little iron gate creaked on rusty hinges. The temple building looked terribly old and drapes of rope and prayer flags hung from the beautifully carved balustrades high up under the roof.

The well kept track led us into and through some of the most scenic forests we have seen so far. Greens of all shades; sun streaking through the trees; tall, straight trunks crusted with bark; and through the gaps in these woodland giants stretched wide open views of marching blue ridges capped with distant, snowy peaks. I felt the space of the place and relaxed. We washed and drank from cold, crystal mountain streams that splashed down over the track and, looking up, my face dripping and my head cooled, I gazed out at the country through which we are running. This is the stuff from which memories are made.

Day Sixty-one. This morning my bowels hit home once again. Four times I had to stop, four times in the first hour of running. My stomach churned away on overtime and I think I've got a nasty cut down in the nether regions which may be going septic. This continual diarrhoea only exacerbates the problem. My stomach just does not like Indian food, it's as simple as that. We had a good laugh about it though. I mean, of all the likely injuries one should sustain when running the Himalayas, a cut nether region is hardly the one that springs to mind. It's amazing just how debilitating such a thing can be. Aside from the embarrassment and the funny walk, I can't laugh, cough, finish a pee properly, sit down heavily or wipe my bottom without an excruciating stab of pain. It's no laughing matter.

We ran down off the ridge, over the bridge, over the river at a grotty little stop called Lori, and then climbed steadily north up the dirt road aiming for Ani village. We were on the side of a steep gorge, and far below a small river tumbled over boulders. All around us, the green but rocky slopes reared vertically up into the sky, where the clouds were slowly gathering.

As we chatted and joked together, the kilometre posts soon passed and after a relatively short day of twenty-two miles, we reached Ani with time to spare. It began to rain.

We huddled in a tiny, dark tea shop, sipping mango juice and watching the rain get heavier and heavier until it poured down in a continuous sheet. Everyone has run for shelter and battened down the hatches of their little stores. The rain hammers on corrugated roofs, pours in streams off eaves, and a few drops trickle down the back of my neck through a hole in the roof.

The hut is packed with people sheltering from the rain. Everyone is soaked through and the heat from the fire causes steam to rise from wet clothing and the dank smell of it fills the hut. A fly has landed in my mango juice. It struggles briefly against the thick orange liquid then dies. I hope the rain stops soon.

After a while, the storm eases and, donning full rain suits we venture out to look for somewhere to stay the night. The little village sits squashed up against the sides of the valley. A small river rushes down from the heights to meet the main flow of water pouring down the gorge up which we have been travelling. This is the last stop before the Jalori Pass, 4,000 feet up and twenty miles away to the west. The village, a jumbled collection of mud and wood shacks, lives for the dirt track that acts as a road. The track brings trucks heading up and down, to and from the pass, and Ani has become the drivers' rest stop. A small concrete bridge straddles the river that rushes white and frothing over its steep, rock-strewn bed.

I was standing on this bridge when it happened.

The cry went up . . . 'landslide, landslide.' People suddenly started to race out of every door and hatchway and rush to the banks of the river. Excitement and fear filled the air as the whole village crowded onto the bridge or climbed onto vantage points. They were staring up river. Something was happening. Something big, but what? A loud, excited shouting from the people standing on the hillside above me. They were pointing up the narrow river valley and I followed their gaze.

Something was moving, something frightening, something huge and brown and boiling. I strained my eyes to see, and suddenly it became clear. Upriver, not 400 yards away, an enormous, frothing, angry, brown mash of mud and water was crashing down towards the village. It was unbelievable and frightening as hell. The river was being drowned with mud. This ten-foot-high, moving mass of living hell crashed over boulders, and trees were smashed down and pushed ahead of the raging, mountainous torrent like matchsticks. A noise like thunder crescendoed and the ground beneath my feet trembled with the force. I had never seen anything like this: a huge mudslide in full flow, awesome in its destructive power. It smashed down under the bridge, carrying five-ton boulders before it and leaving them suspended on the banks. Mud, thick and brown, spattered everything and coated the boulders of the river with its sticky mess. The noise was deafening as the boiling river of death sucked and roared and threw itself headlong down the valley. Nothing could have stopped this monster, nothing, for I was seeing nature at its most powerful and most destructive. I shall never forget it!

The scene on the banks was one of frantic activity. After the villagers had recognised the size of the slide, they rushed into their homes to remove any valuable belongings. The mud had risen up nearly to the top of the banks and it was tearing at the bridge with enormous power. Everything could go at any second. No-one stood on the bridge now, frightened that they would end up like the drowned oxen that the mud brought crashing down past the village. A man would last only seconds in this fury: it would pick him up and hurl him downstream, smashing him to mincemeat against rocks and boulders.

Justin dashed around taking photographs and if he got too close to the edge, the watching villagers would yell at him to get back. He had forgotten his sore knees and aching limbs. The excitement of the slide gave him a new energy and he bounced around the banks clicking away, seemingly uncaring of the danger.

Then slowly and almost imperceptibly the power began to fade and the danger of collapsing banks and bridges disappeared. The frantic activity of people emptying their homes ceased and we all just stood around and watched the river of mud churning thick and brown, a seemingly endless flow of liquid death that would slowly peter out over the next few hours. We stood and stared, numbed by the experience.

Overleaf: Mudslide

To the villagers of Ani, the mudslide was part of the cycle that makes up their lives. Some of them had stood and watched as their small fields, hard-fought from the rocky soil, were destroyed in the blink of an eye. Others had lost cattle, a vital source of income for the family. But no people had been killed this time. Three days earlier and further down the gorge three shepherds, sheltering under a rock on the nearly dry riverbed, had been swept away by another smaller mudslide. Their bodies were recovered two days later, several miles down the gorge. They were virtually unrecognisable.

This time, the people of Ani had been lucky. But the mudslides have happened before and they will happen again.

The mudslide remained uppermost in our minds as we ran on for the next three days towards Manali. It was an example of just how suddenly death can appear in this part of the world. Beneath our feet, the Himalayas are always being pushed higher and higher by titanic forces that melt rock and shake the land. Above us, the weather lashes the ground, changing its shape and carving rock and ice into valleys and cliffs. When the precarious balance tips, an extra drop of rain, a stronger wind, or a snowflake, avalanches crash down the mountains and landslides tear away a millenium of nature's work. In amongst this power, mankind is tiny and insignificant and lives are snuffed out in an instant. Up here in the Himalayas, the Indian people may build roads and bridges and attempt to tame the power of nature, but the land will always remain supreme. Bridges are washed away, roads are covered by snow and rendered useless and earthquakes and mudslides destroy towns and villages.

It is this raw power that I find so stimulating and so satisfying, and it brings home to me just how temporary I am; how temporary we all are, on this earth. The more I experience of this sort of thing, the more I feel the need to use every day of my life and not to waste a moment.

On Day Sixty-four we ran hot and sweating up to the head of the Beas river valley and into the town of Manali. Amazingly, we were ten days ahead of schedule.

Chapter 17

TURNING BACK

'Last time I was here,' said Justin, 'it was sleeting and the temperature was well below zero.'

We were safely ensconced in a hotel on the edge of the town. We had showered, shaved and donned our new socks and shoes, which Justin had picked up from the Mayo Restaurant, where he had left them back in February.

'It was pretty miserable then,' he continued. 'Dark, cold and very few people here.'

'As I remember it, I was supping G and Ts in the British Embassy in Delhi at the time. That was pretty tough too you know,' I taunted.

We grinned at each other, both thoroughly pleased to be here, and ahead of time too.

But although we were ahead of schedule and cheery because of it, we were both desperately tired and sore. We had been on the move for sixty-four days now, with only four days' proper rest, and our bodies were giving us painful messages warning us to stop or else. Justin's ankle was now aching, for between Ani and here he had gone over on it, twisting it painfully and causing some swelling; and I was suffering from a twinge in my left knee, which made me wince with pain whenever I was running uphill.

We decided to take an extra day's rest here in Manali, so Day Sixty-five was spent washing kit, writing letters to loved ones back home and gaining information on the route ahead.

From Manali we planned to head north over three high passes, through the Zanskar and into the Kashmir valley. The finish was a mere 300 to 400 miles away and we estimated fifteen days. At the start of the trip, fifteen days had seemed an awfully long time, but now it was an easy enough target to aim for.

But there were problems. We were about to run into the most troubled part of the whole journey so far, for strife-torn Kashmir was only a few days away and the newspaper reports were not good. The province was being torn apart by a nationalistic uprising and the subsequent intervention of the Indian forces. Reports spoke of an Indian army of occupation, killing and imprisoning at random and without trial; of twenty-four-hour curfews in the main centre of Srinagar and the outlying towns, of the Kashmiri People's Liberation Front, an organisation fighting for Kashmir's independence from India which had been responsible for the killing of soldiers and government officials. At this moment a general strike was paralysing the valley and tension on the streets and in the surrounding villages was at breaking point.

Kashmir, being predominantly Muslim, was being supported by Pakistan and there was now talk of war between India and Pakistan over the future of Kashmir. There have been three wars between the two countries, in 1948, 1965 and 1971 and apparently this year the Prime Minister of India, Mr Singh, was quoted as telling the Indian people to 'psychologically prepare themselves for war', while the Pakistan premier, Benazir Bhutto, talked of a 'thousand-year war'. Things were not looking good.

Each side was blaming the other for the current tension. India was claiming that Pakistan was practising 'adventurism' on the issue of Kashmiri independence, and providing training and weapons for Kashmiri 'terrorists'. Pakistan was blaming the Indian government for the troubles, saying that the Muslims were discriminated against, both in the job market and in schools and colleges in Kashmir. The years of neglect and lack of investment in Kashmir by the Indians had caused the disaffection and now they were paying for it.

The whole situation was extremely unstable and in a few days' time Justin and I would be running into the middle of it. As I read all these reports, sitting safely in my hotel, I recalled Adrian Stones of the British Embassy in Delhi. 'Don't go,' he had said, and I began to wonder why we were not taking his advice.

But we had come too far to be stopped now. We got out our rather battered map of the Himalayas and looked back at the hundreds of sweat-soaked miles that lay behind us. 'There's no going back now,' I said.

'Not unless we're in a wooden box,' answered Justin. His determination to finish was matched by his adventurous spirit and he was looking forward to plunging into this unstable land.

My only real fear was of being stopped; of being prevented from completing the run. The finish filled my mind and I dreaded the possibility of being stopped so close to the end. To finish was everything for me. Danger or no danger, I had to get to Gulmarg. On Day Sixty-six we headed north out of Manali, ankles and knees twitching and minds filled with uncertainty about what lay ahead.

Just out of Manali are many little shanty villages that have sprung up by the side of the road. The people living here work either on the road or in labouring jobs in the town itself. They live in tiny hovels made of stone, plastic sheeting and flattened, rusting metal boxes that once held cooking oil. It seems such a pity that even here in this beautiful valley, there is this fatal attraction for people of the hills. They come from their remote villages seeking work and money. They get only a little work, exploitative wages, and disease from the terribly insanitary conditions in which they live. It's a sorry sight.

We strode on and up. High above were snowy peaks and enormous cliffs of jagged rock. Fir trees clung to every slope and green and yellow signs by the side of the road told us to 'plant a tree, save a life'. The sun came out and, as we trudged up a shortcut, a near-vertical tiny track leading up to the zig-zagging road, I looked around me and smiled a satisfied smile. It was a beautiful place to be. Mountains, snow, cascading torrents, huge cliffs, trees glowing bright green in the sunlight and a blue sky. I forgot about my sweating effort and eased into the slope.

The road deteriorated as we climbed, and soon it was just a pitted dirt track. It twisted and turned wildly up the valley, making huge zigging detours round rocky buttresses before zagging back on course again. The pass is 6,000 feet above Manali, and this height had to be gained in just a short distance. We tried cutting directly off near-vertical slopes in an effort to lessen the distance but from below it is difficult, or more often impossible, to see where the main track cuts across the slope above us. The trees, rocks and perspective all blur one's vision. But today luck was on our side and our shortcuts worked.

After several hours, we were above the snow-line and trudging ankle-deep through the white crust. At Mahri, we stared aghast at the jumble of makeshift shelters that had been built by the side of

the road. At this time of year this is as far as the bulldozers can get
for the sheer quantity of snow beats even them until the melt at the
end of May. Here, Indian holidaymakers get lifts up by Land Rover
and come to play in the snow. You can hire Wellington boots, skis,
a cart on skis and buy all sorts of snack-type food. People shout and
laugh and ski and throw snowballs.

We shovelled bread and a greasy meat soup down our gullets
then, leaving the giggling holidaymakers behind, we squared our
shoulders and headed up for the pass.

Kicking steps in the snow with our running shoes, we climbed
high and all around us the peaks, glaciers and icy cliffs became
clear. As we reached the top at 12,700 feet, a vast blue sky was
rapidly turning very grey as an approaching storm threatened. At
this point we left the warm and tree covered India that we had
come to know so well and entered the cold barrenness of the
Lahoul Spiti region.

Setting off at a run across the snow, we soon found ourselves
sliding at incredible pace down the steep north side of the pass. Just
barely in control we whooped and shouted with exhilaration as we
flew, slid and fell down the slope. This was fell-running in the snow
at its best. The air whipped past our faces, our legs went in all
directions, arms flailed about wildly, there were crazy grins on our
faces and we just let ourselves go. When we fell, it was a soft
landing. Fantastic, exhilarating stuff.

Half an hour and two thousand feet down, we stood sweating
and panting in a very different world. The sky was now an angry
grey and it had begun to rain. No trees were in sight, just grey rock
and dirty snow. Where had all the green gone? My knee was giving
me major gyp. During our crazed descent, it had been fine as the
going was soft and fluid, but in our excitement we had missed the
partially snow-covered track and ended up too low. Now, as we
traversed the rocky, snow-strewn slope, the pain returned with a
vengeance and I slowed right down, trying to take care to put my
foot flat each time. Not the easiest of tasks on a snowy slope of
forty-five degrees with a roaring, icy, grey river 500 feet below.

The surrounding country had an untamed, ferocious beauty
about it that reminded me of parts of north-western China and I
had always imagined that the Hindu Kush and the Karakoram
would look like this. It is difficult to believe that anything could live

Climbing high up towards the Rhotang Pass

here, and yet the people do scrape a living from the rocky soil and, because their crops are harvested at a different time of year from the rest of India, they can get extremely good prices. At this time of year, everything is carried over the high passes when the weather is good, but in a month or so, the snow will have melted sufficiently to allow vehicles over and then the pace of trade will increase.

In the early evening we trudged wetly into the quiet little village of Sissu. There were a few grey, square houses, no shops and a few red-faced Tibetan children scampering about. They screamed in terror as we approached, and rushed off to hide in their mothers' skirts. An old man with a bristly grey growth on his chin found us a room in an ancient white building on the edge of the village. The room was very cold and smelled of neglect. We sat, huddled in our sleeping bags and duvet jackets, drawing patterns in the dust on the table and thinking of home.

The following morning dawned grey and cold and drizzly and as we set off, with only a half-litre of chlorinated water to sustain us, we buttoned our rainsuits to the neck and followed the Chandra River downstream.

I am feeling tired and sore today. I woke this morning with a painful left kneecap, a twinge in my left foot and a worsening shin splint on my right leg. Added to all of this is the ever-present bowel problem, so I am not the happiest of men at the moment. I put on as brave a face as I can manage and shuffle on.

At the tiny wayside halt of Tandi, we leave the Chandra flowing west and cut north-east up the Bhaga River, which will lead us up towards the Shingo La, our next major pass and the high gateway to Kashmir.

As we run and stagger up the valley it becomes gorge-like, and huge fields of scree and snow surround us while far below, the river, white and angry, slashes at the rock with gritty fury. Erosion plays a powerful and never-ending part in shaping this land. Mankind tries hard to tame it but eventually the land reclaims its own. Roads disappear in landslides, bridges fall into rivers, and dams are busted by earth tremors. Up here in this remote, barren country we feel very close to nature and all that she can throw at us. The sheer immensity of the mountains dwarfs us, and we move like two tiny ants over a ploughed field.

Twenty miles further on, the town of Kyelong appears: a jumbled collection of grey concrete-block houses, perched on two levels on the side of the valley, high above the river. In the centre, the school, a white, pagoda-like building, looks quite out of place in amongst the wet and the mud that covers the streets. A few shops, busy with traders and customers, ply a trade in spare parts for vehicles, sweetmeats and onions fried in batter, and an assortment of everyday hardware needs. People huddle from the rain under eaves and use the time to talk and eat or drink tea from tiny glasses. Everyone here looks Tibetan. They are small and round and solidly built. Tough men with thick wrists and stubby fingers, faces worn a deep, wrinkled brown by the sun. The women are colourfully dressed and, as we approach, their broad faces break into beaming, toothy smiles. It must be a bloody hard living out here, yet they are polite and cheery. What a change from the generally surly Indians and Himachal Pradesh. Kyelong in the rain is a rather depressing place, despite the bustling activity and, having filled up on samozas, potatoes and *daal* we are glad to move on.

Self conscious Tibetan girls in Lahoul Spiti (north-west India)

We passed groups of people working their tiny fields, little patches of brown and green almost hidden by the grey and white of rock and snow. They hacked away at the thin soil with pickaxes and hoes; planting potatoes or peas; irrigating the fields by digging ditches to channel water, and collecting firewood. Up here, where trees are extremely scarce, they grow a certain type of tree specifically for firewood. The tree is pruned regularly and eventually a thick bush of branches forms at the top of its eight-foot-high trunk. The more the tree is pruned, the more wood it produces. It's an ingenious system that leaves the people self-sufficient and self-supporting in firewood.

We also spotted a micro-hydro-electric installation, funded by Indian government money, and providing electricity for the local area. The countryside is ideal here for this sort of power generation, with steep slopes and roaring rivers. Our friends at Intermediate Technology would have had a field day.

Evening found us ensconced in a dark and dirty little backroom behind a wayside *chai* house at Gemur, yet another depressing little grey cluster of concrete blocks. It was cold and, huddled snug in our sleeping bags on the floor, we listened to the quiet scratching of mice as they scurried around in the dark. I remembered a story two friends of mine had told me of a trip of theirs to Nepal a few years ago. They had been walking in some remote part of western Nepal and had laid out their bags for the night in a little shed. The locals had warned them of rats and they were very aware of the continued existence of bubonic plague in parts of the country. They had gone to bed with their sleeping bags pulled tight so that only their noses were poking through and had lain awake all night listening to the vermin rooting around the hut and feeling them running over their prostrate bodies. I checked the drawstring of my bag was pulled tight and slept.

Day Sixty-eight dawned clear and bright and we ran out of the village into a freshening breeze and under a bright blue sky. My shin was already painful but I seemed to be able to go at a decent enough pace and the pain was at least only intermittent.

In an hour and a half we had reached Darcha, our launching point for the Shingo La. The village comprised two tiny shops selling tea, potatoes and a few stale packets of biscuits, and a cluster of low workmen's huts, inhabited only in the summer months and now lying empty. There were just ten people here, huddled inside one of the shops, drinking tea and playing card games. We gathered some information on the nature of the pass and of the condition of the snows. Our map showed a track running up the right side of the Barai Nala River then another smaller path cutting north up a side valley to the pass. Alas, the map was nearly useless as the scale was just too large, and the information we had gathered from the people here in Darcha was also unreliable. They do not venture up high at this time of year and so all comments were based on wild guesses, although we did not know this at the time. The pass is open to people and animals in July, and we were here in the middle of May, yet the advice was positive enough for us to give it a go.

Having filled ourselves to the gunnels with boiled potatoes and hot tea, we set off up the slope into the most remote and empty part of India we had yet experienced.

Four miles further on we passed the small farm houses of Rarig and Chika; then we were alone. The path shrank to a sheep track and we found ourselves skirting the side of forty-five degree scree slopes. My shin had now become painful to the touch and even more nasty when moving. I soaked an elasticated bandage in an icy stream and put it over the offending muscle. Our little track dipped down to a tiny gorge, where the river surged green and frothy through a small gap in the cliffs and we had to shout to be heard. It was here that the fun started. The track had disappeared. Ahead lay fields of snow and scree and huge jumbles of boulders four storeys high. Justin had seen some people in a remote field further down the valley and he went off in search of directions. I sat on the boulder-strewn valley floor, dwarfed by the surrounding mountains, and contemplated my leg. The pain by now was very bad indeed and there seemed no let up. The terrain ahead of us promised a hard climb and at high altitude as well. I knew that if we could get within striking distance of the pass that night, then I could stand the pain in order to get over this, our last main gateway to success.

Justin arrived, having found the people he'd seen earlier, but they spoke no English and he had had major communication difficulties. From what he could gather, the path led up the left side of the river then crossed over further up. But we did not know where the hell the path was in the first place. It was lost in the jumble of rocks and under snow. We had to pick as good a route as possible.

For hours, we struggled and stumbled and slipped and fell through snowdrifts and negotiated huge boulder fields. The going was the roughest I have ever known. There was no track, just huge pressure ridges of rock and boulders. We went up and down; our legs were so very tired and our lungs gasped in the thinning air. It began to snow and the sun was hidden by clouds. A fresh wind blew at our chests. We traversed snow slopes, on which the snow had softened during the day, and too often we'd fall through up to our waists. The effort was exhausting us. My legs felt like dead weights and we seemed to be covering the ground so slowly. We thought one mile an hour was about right. Justin led all the way up the valley and I plodded behind, my leg screaming at me to stop, the pain taking as much energy as the journey itself. I tried thinking of good things, of my wife, our plans for the future, of good food and comfortable surroundings. Anything to make the pain go away. But it was always there. Like a living thing it growled and spat with every step I took. I was not having a good time.

After several hours, we struggled to the top of yet another mountain of boulders and there in the distance was a bridge over the river – at least it had once been a bridge. Only the two uprights remained and a fraying rope ran between them over the freezing green water below. Up above the ruined bridge was a gorge-like valley, at the bottom of which was a river running down to join the Barai Nala. Was this our turn-off? It could have been. It was heading in the right direction, but it looked so narrow and almost vertical. There was no track visible anywhere on the other side.

We waded through slushy snow towards the bridge, sinking to our knees into the wet underneath. Was it our valley or wasn't it? We just didn't know. Surely we couldn't have come far enough yet; but why would there be a bridge here? There was no track anywhere; but the bridge was heading in the right direction. Wasn't the slope too steep for anything to get up there? These were the questions we asked ourselves as we sat, feet frozen to numbing blocks of ice and faces a ruddy red from the head-wind. It was decision time. We decided to move on up the valley until we rounded the next spur, from where we could look again at the situation. The weather was worsening slowly and ahead of us lay more of the same for many miles. We were both as tired as we'd ever been and now the added quandary of whether or not we were on the right route increased the pressure on us. We felt terribly alone and vulnerable.

An hour and a half later, the end of the spur had joined another spur and there seemed no end to our torture in sight. We were terribly cold and disillusioned. I stood and stared up the valley. Everything was grey and barren and we were lost at altitude in a dangerous and remote place. At our earlier discussion by the ruined bridge, one of the options had been to turn back. Justin, although physically the stronger of us at this time, had been more in favour of this option and now, standing there in the cold and the snow, staring up this godforsaken valley, I knew he was right. He had only gone on from the bridge because I had been so adamant about not turning back and now, having broken trail for hours, he looked exhausted. The tears of frustration welled up in my eyes and I turned away and said, 'Let's go back.' With those three words, I saw my dream of running the Himalayas in a hundred days disappearing. For two years I had planned and dreamed of this trip and now here we were, turning our backs on the route west. The tears stung my eyes and I choked with frustration and utter depression. I put on my glasses to hide from Justin just how upset I was and followed his wavering steps back down the way we had come.

For four-and-a-half hours we kept moving up and down over the same boulder-strewn slopes and slippery snow fields. My leg was very painful and I trudged on, eyes half-closed, just wishing it was all over. The sun disappeared behind the mountains and we continued on in the dark. The track was just a pale, dark blur on the hillside as we reached the tiny bridge over the gorge and stumbled on, very slowly now, to the farmhouse at Chika. Rounding a bend at half eight, we saw light blazing from the windows of the *dhobi* mud-house. It was the most welcome sight I have ever seen. We knocked on the door and called out and were finally allowed in. Two very tired and sore Himalayan runners collapsed on the rugs in the corner of a warm room. The fire blazed and the tea was hot. We had been going for fourteen hours and at last the day's ordeal was over.

We slept like dead men that night and did not stir until our tiny watch alarms bleeped at us at half past five this morning. The farmer, in whose home we were staying, had eleven children, two of whom had recently died. He and the rest of his family farmed this sparse land and carted the crops off to the road on the backs of horses and mules. They were terribly poor in material possessions yet immensely rich in human kindness and compassion. Last night we had arrived, wet, cold and miserable and in the pitch black of night, two complete strangers. And yet, they had welcomed us in and had shared with us their meal of tea and *tupa*, a simple flour and vegetable soup. The farmer would not even accept any money. Their generosity and trust was heart-warming indeed.

My right shin is really very painful and I suspect either a ripped tendon or a fractured shin-bone. I have obviously completely overdone the injury and now cannot walk or stand without help. The only recourse is to rest. Time will tick on by while I do so but we are at least ahead of schedule, so maybe we can still make it. It all seems so unfair that this should happen now, in sight of the end. Success now teeters on the knife-edge of injury. If only I didn't feel so bloody useless.

Justin is also very tired and obviously disappointed about my condition. He is taking it in his usual calm and patient way and is immensely supportive. He found me a stick and, having thanked the farmer, we hobbled slowly back down the valley. I could only move at a snail's pace and it was soon obvious that no attempt could be made on the pass for a good few days. Justin left me to make my excruciating way down the track and set off on his own for Rarig to try and get a horse for me to ride down to the road at Darcha. The more I walked the more I aggravated the injury and the longer it would take to heal. I was dying to take my weight off it and any form of transport would have been welcome. We figured that we had already come by foot over this terrain and therefore to back track by other means would not detract from our achievement.

By the time I reached Rarig, Justin had found a trusty steed. The beast, a dirty grey and rather knackered-looking animal, stood quietly beside him, its head hung low. Justin had a huge grin on his face and was obviously very pleased with himself. 'Come on then, Clint,' he said. 'Hop up on here and we'll be down in no time.'

'Well done, that man,' I answered, thoroughly pleased that I would not have to keep walking. 'You're a bloody marvel.'

'Well, we've got to pay for it, but it looks gentle enough,' he said, looking sideways at Noddy, who looked to be at least 150 years old.

'But I haven't got a licence,' I murmured.

Our little procession set off for Darcha. The young son of the farmer at Rarig led the way, pulling Noddy by the leading rein, while I sat high and ungainly in the saddle, clutching on for dear life, and Justin carried our two packs, one on his back and the other on his head. Noddy lurched, my bottom grew numb and my legs set into what I feared would be a permanent bow. I had never realised that riding a horse could be so damn uncomfortable, but the weight was off my leg and that was all that mattered. The ride down to Darcha took two hours and ruined my sex-life forever . . . oh well! By the end of the day, we had hailed the only vehicle which had passed, and were now back in Kyelong, recuperating.

We stayed at Kyelong for five days, five whole days of no movement. The frustration and uncertainty about the future were awful but there was nothing else we could do.

Justin was a real brick. In his position I would have been chomping at the bit and impatient to get on. But he looked after me very well indeed and kept himself busy into the bargain. He found a stick, a horse and a jeep yesterday. Today, Day Seventy, he found me a doctor. Apparently there is a small hospital here, the only one for sixty miles in any direction, and the doctor, a black-haired, slightly balding and rather severe-looking Tibetan man in his forties, is keen to move to one of the cities on the plains to specialise in sports injury.

He probed around and, after I had issued forth several loud yells as he found sensitive spots, he informed me that I had a ripped tendon. He gave me anti-inflammatory drugs and told me to bathe the leg in hot, salty water three times a day.

The days passed terribly slowly and the pain became more localised, so I could now pinpoint the trouble spot. I hobbled off to see the doctor at his tiny hospital. After I had waited an hour and a half for him and his friends to finish their game of table tennis I was ushered into the hospital ward. What a place! Straight out of Florence Nightingale's era. Rusty old metal bedsteads, and thin, red mattresses that puffed a cloud of dust into the air whenever anyone sat on them. It was dark and dirty and there were the blanketed forms of those more unfortunate than I huddled in coughing or silent lumps, suffering whatever wretched illness had befallen them.

Bottles of antiseptic lotion sat on grimy bedside tables. The contents of one had dribbled and coagulated down the side of the bottle and made a dark yellow stain on the woodwork underneath. An old peasant lady lying on one of the beds watched me with curious but nearly lifeless eyes as I hobbled in and sat on one of the empty beds. A group of ladies in Tibetan dress and one in a *sari* were chatting away in an adjoining room.

When the doctor and I appeared, there was a bustle of activity from all except the one in the *sari* who continued nonchalantly filing her nails. Suddenly I was the centre of attention. A small white tray with a very large pair of forceps, some surgical gloves, a needle and a syringe was placed on the bed beside my now bare and outstretched leg. The needle was not in any sort of sterile dressing, it just sat there in the tray picking up germs. My mind turned to thoughts of infectious diseases, AIDS being the one that first sprang to mind. If they were going to inject me I would insist on seeing a sterile needle being used.

The doctor then prodded around the offending part of my anatomy, found the sensitive bit and I yelled.

'Well,' he said, 'I was going to inject hydrocortisone between the tendon and bone, but it could be that you have a fracture of the bone instead, and not a torn tendon at all.'

Ed suffering on crutches

'Oh that's bloody great!' Sitting up supported by my hands, I hung my head back and felt like screaming.

'We have no solution to develop the x-ray pictures here,' continued the doctor, 'but hopefully tomorrow some will arrive and we will x-ray your leg to see whether there is a fracture or not.'

Nothing to do until tomorrow then.

I hobbled, painfully slowly, back to the hotel, my mind racing. What if it is broken? Will it get worse? Can I stand the pain for another 250 miles? Why can't I just be satisfied with stopping here? But I know I won't be satisfied, can't be satisfied until I reach Gulmarg.

I met Justin back in the hotel and explained the situation. After the x-ray tomorrow, we must go on. I would try and find some crutches and, leg or no leg, we would finish what we had started. The best thing would be for him to stay ahead then I would have to keep going, just to catch him. It would be a good incentive. He was in complete agreement and was obviously happy that we were to be off again.

'I've found another route through to Kashmir, Ed.' His eyes burned with excitement. 'I think we can make it without crossing the Shingo La. It's a route that should give your leg a chance to heal a little as there are more tracks.'

'Show me; where do you mean?'

'Well, if we head west from here we can follow more valleys and more valleys mean more people and therefore better trade routes. By the time we get to the main passes your leg should have mended some.' We whipped out the map, a sudden rush of hope filled our minds and, as we plotted out the new route, our excitement mounted.

'We can still do it,' I said. 'We can make the hundred days. Justin, you're a bloody marvel.'

Our new route would take us south of our original one, planned back in Britain, but it was definitely the most sensible course of action for us. We had a responsibility to people back home and to our friends at Intermediate Technology, who were expecting great things of us. To head up into the lonely, empty Zanskar with a suspected fractured leg and to end up frozen stiff and dead would not do anyone, least of all ourselves, any good at all. So now we would move west via Kilar to Kishtwar then north-west into the Kashmir valley and thence to Gulmarg.

Tomorrow I would have the x-ray; then on Day Seventy-five we would be off again. An interesting time lay ahead. Until now it had always been me pushing us on, leading and providing the drive. Now the tables were turned. Justin was the stronger of the two of us and I hoped he would enjoy being in front for once, pulling us on towards the finish.

It's amazing really that the two of us have got so far together. In

Peru in 1985, we couldn't stand to be alone together for more than an hour or so before we'd be flying at each other's throats. Now, only five years later, here we are, having lived cheek-by-jowl since early February and still together. Of course we have our differences: two people could hardly be more different; and yet our experiences bind us together. There are arguments, usually over silly things; there are silent moments when I'm sure we are both quietly cursing the other for a thoughtless remark or deed, but these moments pass and we are laughing and discussing and theorising and planning together again.

On Day Seventy-four I went off for my x-ray while Justin searched out a pair of crutches. The x-ray unit was a sight to behold. No polished floors or protective screens; just a dirty old room with a dusty concrete floor and a simple x-ray machine mounted on a tripod over a table. The windows were boarded up with bits of cardboard, mud and flattened tin containers, while broken panes of glass lay splintered on the ground underneath. Outside the door, on the long, covered porchway, were three or four dishes, some flat, some round, and a metal bucket. All these dishes had different-coloured liquids in them – the acids and other chemicals for the developing of the x-ray prints. I was introduced to the young, half-shaven and rather dishevelled young man who stood amongst these chemicals, his hands stained a disturbing shade of white, and was told he would take care of me. I waited in line. There was a soldier with a broken finger, a woman whose painful wincing whenever she breathed indicated a fractured rib and a young girl with her mother, who also had something wrong with her chest.

At last it was my turn. Shoes and socks off, I got up onto the table. My foot was carefully placed on the x-ray plate by the young man with the stained hands, then the ominous and, I could now see, rather ancient x-ray camera was positioned over the offending part, and the pictures were taken. I put my shoes and socks back on and limped outside into the sun to wait for the results. Out came the stained young man a few minutes later, holding three prints, one for each of his patients. He plunged the prints into a blue liquid and then plunged his hands in afterwards. Acid and other unknown chemicals were then splashed around and there was the developed picture. I moved in from my vantage point several yards away, where I was waiting out of reach of the splashing acid, and took my x-ray. No broken bone . . . yippee!

So, tendonitis it is, painful it will be, but better it will get, ideally before Gulmarg. Justin came up trumps with the crutches and I went and had the tops of them padded to minimise the discomfort and friction under my arms.

Tomorrow we will be on our way again.

'Those Himalayas in the mind are not so easily
possessed:
There's more than precipice and storm between
you and your Everest.'
   C. Day Lewis

Chapter 18

DON'T LET ME STOP

Day Seventy-five: the roaring, grey river valley down which we are travelling narrows into a steep gorge. The water thunders unseen far below, then emerges again, angry and frothing, as the valley widens once more. The Himalayas tower around us and waterfalls freefall hundreds of feet over black cliffs.

The road was mostly tarmac, the smooth surface broken at irregular intervals by stony track that made the going hard for me with my crutches. At the start of the day I had a localised pain in my shin but with the aid of the crutches I could hammer along at a fair pace. After an hour, the first blisters started to appear on my hands and the underneath of my arms began to take a real bashing from putting all my weight on the top of the crutches. Where the ground was rough I frequently 'caught a crab' with the crutches. Whenever this happened my hands smashed against the handles and the blisters groaned. I felt as though I was being battered to death. My biceps and forearms and wrists pumped up with the effort, and when I took my hands off the crutches it took a few seconds for them to straighten out again. I did not have a whole lot of fun that day.

We made twenty-seven miles in a long, long day with only one short stop for water and tasteless glucose biscuit. The gathering darkness of night found us in the large village of Udaipur. It was cold and a fierce wind filled the air with dust and rattled wooden shutters. As the candle here in our dingy little room burned itself down to nothing, I crawled numb and exhausted into my sleeping bag. Tomorrow would be another day.

Day Seventy-six. By midday today I have caught so many 'crabs' that I've lost count. The tarmac has disappeared and a wide, rocky, broken path has taken its place. Occasionally a freezing river cascades down over the cliffs and floods the track. As Justin trips nimbly over the rocks, avoiding wet feet, I relish the cold water easing the burning in my shin and wade through, the crutches becoming excellent stabilisers in the torrent. My shoulders, arms and hands feel as battered and sore as if I have been hit by a rugby scrum and I'm not really enjoying myself.

Here at Tandi, we rest and suck on our water bottles. It has been a long and lonely journey here, with nowhere to stop since we left Udaipur. The fir trees are back again, cloaking the slopes with a rich green and in sheltered gullies, small glaciers drip into the swirling grey waters of the Chenal River.

Sitting with Justin, in the shade of a broad tree outside a small hut, we make an effort to find out about the route ahead from five Indian men who are resting here as well. They are curious about the crutches and shake their heads and waggle their fingers at me. Each of them has a walking stick and it seems that they are advising me to use sticks instead of the crutches. It sounds like a good idea and I'm pretty fed up with the damn crutches anyway. I cannot use them when going downhill as I fall over on my face if the angle is too steep. With a couple of sticks I might be able to take my weight more efficiently. Justin found an axe, which was not difficult as we are in a forestry area, and cut two chest-high lengths of wood for me. I whittled down the handled end and wrapped some of our precious sticky bandage round the top so I wouldn't get splinters.

The remainder of the day passed in a blur of twisting track that climbed and dropped as it traversed this enormous valley. The end of the day found us at Raoli, a forestry workers' stop. The men here (there are no women) are rough and simple but they smile easily and have given us somewhere to sleep for the night. The filth is disgusting but makes little or no impression on us now for we are well attuned to life in the Himalayas. I managed to wash clothes and body and then sat and stuck pins in my blistered hands and used some of our precious antiseptic cream to prevent infection. The sticks seem to have served their purpose, for there is less pain in my shin and now, at the end of the day, it is still swollen but I can hobble around well enough. Could it be on the mend at last?

Day Seventy-seven. We covered twenty-seven miles today and the sticks are definitely making things easier. The track has, in many places, been ripped away by landslide or covered by mini-glaciers, and crutches would have been worse than useless in this terrain. Watching Justin up ahead slipping and sliding over jumbles of rock and snow, I was glad for the added security of my sticks.

The villages were few and far between and the country was perfect for running. I felt like a frustrated racehorse, longing to plunge through this magnificent scenery at speed. But run I could not. Stagger and plod I could, and I did so as fast as my injury would allow.

The sun blazed from a flawless blue sky and as I stumbled into the ridge-top village of Kilar, where my partner sat waiting, I knew that I was getting better. I was half an hour behind him and, for the first time since Kyelong, he looked as knackered as me.

Day Seventy-eight. Leaving Kilar at half past five this morning, we were not long out of the village when we came across boxes of explosives sitting in large piles on the trackside. A number of them were open and the sticks of dynamite sat exposed to the early morning sun. There was nobody about guarding this destructive pile and we wondered just how long it had been sitting there.

We climbed, then dropped steeply into hidden re-entrants where raging torrents of icy white water wore jagged rock into smooth boulders. We teetered over these rivers on precariously balanced logs then climbed again, hot and sweaty, our legs groaning with the effort. The tiny villages passed by. Dharwas, Shopu, Ishtahari. The way was never obvious but we were lucky to find enough local people travelling between the villages to ensure continual updates on direction.

Justin was way ahead and there came a point when, high up on a ridge and looking down, I could see my partner's tiny jogging figure far, far away through a break in the trees. I was tired, sore and pissed-off in the extreme. Throwing caution to the wind, I hefted my sticks so that I now carried them horizontally, then ran. My shin flared and threatened to pop out of my skin. My knees creaked and groaned, but I was angry. Angry at being injured, angry at being in pain, angry at being so slow, and angry at being behind.

My anger and frustration made me carefree and careless too. I flew down the precipitous slopes, pounded up the steep sides of the spurs and simply creamed along. I didn't care any more if I hurt myself. I was too close to the end to stop now. By the time Justin reached the village of Soarr I had caught up and, although terribly sore, I felt strong and raring to go.

Justin saw me coming and his eyes widened in surprise. We sat on the flat mud roof of a house and ate mountains of chapatis and *daal* and drank two litres of water each in order to rehydrate. I was full of the joys of having run again after what seemed an age of being injured.

'Oh no,' said Justin with a twinkle in his eye. 'Does this mean I'm going to find myself behind again?'

'With the way you're running, matey, I very much doubt it. But I have to admit that I think I've got my confidence back. We are going to make that one hundred days' target, you know.' I felt on top of the world.

'Unless we get arrested in Kashmir, of course,' cautioned Justin. 'I forgot to tell you. We're in Kashmir already. One of those torrents back there marks the boundary. I'm pretty sure we'll be OK up here. It's in the valley itself that all the trouble is occurring.'

Refreshed with the food and liquid, we hacked over the last six miles of the day and reached the village of Atholi. It was pouring with rain by the time we arrived at about six o'clock but we didn't care. It had been a long, hard day.

Atholi is an untidy jumble of mud-built and wooden buildings that sit at the road end. Justin sat in the room playing cards and writing his diary while I sat out on the porch talking with a small group of the local intelligentsia, a bespectacled professor of English, a policeman and a science teacher. The policeman gave me some advice as to what a Kashmiri terrorist looks like.

'He will be bearded and swarthy-looking, will be wearing a baggy shirt and may have one hand held permanently inside the shirt, gripping a gun or a knife ready to slit your throat at a moment's notice.' There was great hilarity all round as he related this description. I hoped he was only kidding.

Day Seventy-nine. Today we met Kashmiri people for the first time. They were herdsmen, travelling with their herds of sheep and long, silky-haired goats. These people are permanently on the move. They have no fixed home, they just go where the grazing is best for their animals. These are Muslim people, similar in appearance to Afghans, such as the *Mujahadeen* (freedom fighters), whom we have seen on our television screens back home. Tall and dark, with bushy beards of black, white or a startling orange, they walk with a loping grace that betrays immense strength and their eyes stare unwaveringly into ours. These are working men with calloused hands and weather-beaten faces, proud men who walk the hills plying a trade that has existed for centuries. Now, of course, boundaries created by foreigners far away limit their movement and dictate to whom they can sell their animals; yet a fierce, independent pride walks with these people and I for one would not fancy taking them on in a scrap.

Huge flocks of animals fill the track and thousands of hooves send clouds of dust up into the air. The men urge and whistle at their beasts and when they see the camera, they are quick to pick up one of their flock and pose proudly for the picture. Their women, hair plaited into long black strands and hanging down over blouses of red and yellow cloth, hide their faces away and keep their distance. The contrast with the Hindu women is striking, for in the Muslim world, women are lower class citizens and must do their masters' bidding.

We travelled for twenty-two miles today and stopped at the wayside halt of Padarna, a dusty collection of wooden shacks and a couple of concrete buildings. The flies covered everything and when lying on the mat, which was my bed for the night, I could feel the dirty little creatures crawling over every exposed piece of skin. The sky turned slowly and imperceptibly from one shade of blue to another until it was black, and the stars pricked the heavens with dotted patterns of light.

During our meal of cold rice and *daal*, which we ate by the flickering light of a paraffin wick lamp, an old Kashmiri man with hollow cheeks and a wispy grey beard started to rant and rave about something or other. It transpired that his rather overbearing wife had thrown him out of the house and he was now lamenting his lot. The old boy must have been at least eighty years old and had resorted to begging for a living. He was treated with much disrespect by the other, younger Kashmiris seated around us, who mocked him, laughed at him and even struck him on the head. It was all a bit embarrassing. He eventually laid himself out on the concrete, covered himself with a blanket and slept, shut off from this cruel world for a few hours.

Day Eighty. A long and seemingly endless twenty-mile shuffle brought us to the hilltop town of Kishtwar, famous for its saffron, and for being a leaping-off-point for trekkers to Kashmir and Lahoul regions.

We had hoped to change some of our traveller's cheques here but the bank would not or could not do it and eventually, after we had hassled the officials sufficiently, a Mr Dev, the local sub-magistrate, gave us 150 rupees in exchange for our only ten-dollar note. We would have to survive on what we had until Srinagar.

Kishtwar, then, as an overnight stop, had suddenly become too expensive so we set off again on tired limbs up the Chatru valley, stopping six miles further on at the 'logging' village of Dudpeath. Here, the Chatru river roars white and clean over its boulder-strewn bed and logs the size of railway sleepers are floated down from upriver and collected here, later to be carted off to Jammu and sold for around 1,100 rupees each. Mr Khosa, a small, round and wrinkled man with smiling eyes, welcomed us to his village and proudly showed us how the logs are winched up from the river and stacked neatly to dry. He was the boss of the whole operation, and not only gave us a bed to sleep on but also had his cook rustle up rice and omelettes for our supper. What a gent!

Day Eighty-one. Our host was up at half past four this morning, badgering his cook into making us chapatis and omelettes. We were fed and away by half past five, touched by this man's generosity and warmth to two total strangers. He wouldn't even accept any money from us.

The track was rough and pitted with holes and twisted and turned a tortuous path up the narrow valley. Now and then, a small community of wooden shacks came and went in the early morning gloom, and only the wisps of smoke filtering through cracks in the roof revealed the presence of people.

At Chingam, the rest of the world was awake and travellers and traders bustled about their business. We sat and ate chapatis and delicious potatoes that tasted uncommonly like the roast potatoes of an English Sunday lunch.

In front of the hut some mules were being loaded up for a journey. Kashmiri men in baggy clothes and sandals were tying on provisions of flour in saddle-bags and colourful rugs, measuring out provisions – of flour, salt, rice, onions, etc. – into huge hessian sacks, donkeys hee-hawed in that ear-piercing, painful way that only donkeys can, men bartered, sat, drank tea, or wandered along to have a look at the foreigners who had just arrived. One toothless old gent with a baggy white turban, brown trousers and days of greying stubble on his chin came and sat at my feet, put a hand on my knee and pleaded to have his photo taken. How could I refuse? He marched into the middle of the dirt track that was the street, shooed everyone else away and stood stiffly to attention, stern-faced, his walking stick clutched at his side as a guardsman clutches his rifle. I took the picture.

Our goal, the Synthan pass, was another 5,000 feet vertically up and twenty-five miles away by track. As we climbed out of the village, the mountains of Kashmir opened up around us and, wiping the sweat from our eyes, we gazed out at all this space, at the snow-covered peaks, the forests, the white, foaming rivers, the green, steep pastures for which Kashmir is so famous and at the blue, blue sky flecked with wispy, fair-weather clouds. Life was good.

We tried to find shortcuts and for a while succeeded in cutting up the spine of a spur and saving ourselves a mile or so of switchbacks. But higher up, the way became littered with fallen trees and their accumulated debris of twisted branches, cones and pine needles. There must have been a gale sometime in the past that created all this destruction and it soon became impossible to move any further up. Trusting our lives to our Reeboks and with our hearts in our mouths we plunged at reckless speed down the side of the slope, aiming for the track that we knew was somewhere below us, hidden in the trees. Slipping on pine needles, we skied down and my sticks became ski poles as I lurched from side to side headlong down the slope.

Back on the track, I gave Justin one of my sticks. 'There's no more need for these,' I said, and with a whoop of glee cast my one far out over the precipice and watched it disappear into the trees below. Justin did the same. My leg was cured.

We 'shuffled' steadily up the track, heading towards the pass, which had now become visible as a distant dip in the mountains up ahead. It never seemed to get any closer, so we decided to ignore it and stop trying to estimate just how far away it was. Our target for the night was Synthan Maiden, marked on our maps as a small village situated just below the main snows of the pass. The track made endless switchbacks and the village was always round the next corner. We became quiet and trudged on in an exhausted silence, each of us lost in our own thoughts and dreaming of a comfortable stop and food in the village.

On dead legs and with drained bodies we rounded one last bend in the track and there, at last, was Synthan Maiden: not a village, nor even a scattered community, but one single white house and empty into the bargain. Locks on the door prevented us entering and we knew we were in for a night out.

High above this building were the indistinct outlines of two huts, and we agreed that that would be where we would stop for the night. As we climbed for forty-five minutes up a steep, green slope, the effort became huge and the breath came in short gasps in the thinning air. Eventually, we collapsed outside what turned out to be two small, simple, open-ended shelters, probably used by herdsmen crossing the pass in summer. It wasn't the Ritz and we had no food or water for our grumbling stomachs, but it was shelter and we were so tired that we really didn't care.

My diary describes our situation:

'I am now sitting high, high above the Chatru valley. I have views of mountains, forests and skies. The only sound is the odd birdsong in the trees far below me and the distant neighing of a horse. There is no-one for miles. We will sleep tonight in this small wooden shelter, with pine-needles as a mattress, and a view that beats any campsite anywhere in the world. Justin has lit and stoked a fire, which crackles and warms just outside the hut in its square of stones. I found an old clay pot and spent some time cleaning it out with snow and pine-needles. We have boiled water now, from melting the snow that lies in patches around about. An empty film packet acts as a ladle and a bit of wire as a handle. I have filtered the boiled, very grey water into a water bottle through my handkerchief and buried the two bottles in the snow to keep them cold. It tastes foul even after all that trouble, but at least we've got something to drink.'

It has been a hard, hard day with a lot of climbing, and tomorrow sees us over the last of the passes of the trip. It feels very much as if something big is coming to an end. This place, this site, this mode of living is so very satisfying and yet I will be glad to have it done.

'Success nourished them; they seemed to be able and so they were able.'
 · Virgil

Chapter 19

TERRORISTS AND TRIUMPH

At four o'clock on Day Eighty-two I woke and watched a thousand tiny blinking stars fading as dawn approached. By five we were up, packed and away. The sun began to peek over the horizon and turned wispy, fair-weather clouds pink then white, and shafts of light bounced off icy black cliffs and snow fields.

After a while, the slope began to level out and we were on the top. The vale of Kashmir, beautiful and strife-torn jewel of the East, opened up before us and, having taken the now obligatory photographs, we plunged down into it. The end was only two-and-a-half days away and we pressed on, running hard and fast over the snows and into pine forests, splashing through crystal streams and boulder-hopping over roaring torrents. We were hungry as hell but couldn't seem to go fast enough. Reluctant to stop for food, we ran straight through the tiny village of Daksum, waving at sleepy faces in doorways and dodging the vicious-looking dogs that padded the track. We carried on past houses made of mud and wood and flattened tin boxes, chickens pecking at seeds thrown to them by an old man, Kashmiri herdsmen, wild-looking, with bushy black beards and staring eyes. Everywhere was suddenly green and lush and the land was flattening right out.

At Vailu, where a small wooden mosque looked down on a smattering of brick buildings, we tucked into a mountain of rice and spicy vegetables and our hunger was satisfied at last. The proprietor of this wayside stop knew a little English and informed us that we were the first foreigners to be seen here this year, for the violence and killing of the past few months had scared any tourists away.

Ed (left) and Justin crossing the final pass of the trip, Synthan Top

There had been general strikes for the last six months that had paralysed the valley's economy and left people hungry for the blood of their Indian oppressors.

'I have only opened two days before now,' he said.

'What do you mean?' asked Justin.

'Before June, everyone on strike, no business, but for June there is agreement with government.' He paused and said, 'We must eat this winter.'

'It seems that we arrived at just the right time then,' said Justin, looking at me with a grin. 'What luck!'

'Luck had nothing to do with it,' I said, tongue in cheek. 'It was all carefully planned.'

'We've caught a sort of window in the conflict. Maybe we won't get arrested after all.'

'God I hope not, not now, surely not now.'

From Vailu, we ran on tired legs down the valley. Both of us were running well, our usual 'shuffling' rhythm eating up the ground and carrying us closer and closer to the finish. In front of us was a huge empty space. The main valley must be that much lower down for I could see only sky ahead. It was the first time that there had been no view, and to us, used to being surrounded by steep slopes, this empty space felt terribly strange. In the valley and out of sight were our two last hurdles, the towns of Anantnag and Srinagar, where most of the killing had taken place. The strong possibility of curfews imposed by the Indian army could add to our troubles, but we would have to wait and see.

At Kokernag, we wangled a room in an empty tourist bungalow for half the usual price and slept as soon as our heads hit the pillows.

Day Eighty-three was a day of long, long, flat and lonely roads. The thin strip of black tarmac stretched far away over the horizon. Trees flanked the roadside, rice paddies glistened wet and green on all sides and far away, on either side of the valley, hazy blue and white mountains encircled the whole.

As we approached the town of Anantnag, the appearance of soldiers became commonplace. Wielding a wide variety of automatic and semi-automatic weapons, they strutted on road bends, entrances and exits to the town and in the town itself. A huge convoy of trucks and jeeps took fifteen minutes to pass, leaving us choking on dust and exhaust fumes. Kashmiri men stared at the drivers of the trucks as they thundered by, and there was hatred and contempt in their eyes. A Kashmiri man slowed his car down and drove beside our plodding figures.

'The Indians are pigs. They should go home. Freedom for Kashmir,' he exclaimed. This he shouted out through the passenger window, as another small convoy swept past in the opposite direction.

Later an Indian soldier drew level on his bicycle. 'Kashmir is for India. We will never give it up. Kashmiri terrorists are evil men and will be given justice.' He cycled off.

'Ever get the feeling you're sitting on a very thin fence?' I said.

'I reckon it's probably the safest place to be at the moment though,' answered Justin.

As we came within half a mile of Anantnag, three soldiers stepped out of the trees by the side of the road and ordered us to stop.

'Get out your papers,' ordered a gruff Indian sergeant with a full black moustache. He held a sub-machine-gun at his waist and there was a magazine in place. We rooted out our passports and the letter from the Indian government and handed them over. The three men, one of whom was an officer, flicked through the pages and read the letter then handed them back to us. The officer, thin and scrawny with a pistol on his belt, told us, 'They are in order,' then he smiled, 'but you cannot go on.'

My heart missed a beat. 'Why not?'

'There is a curfew in Anantnag.'

'But I thought the curfew only lasted at night-time.'

'No, no, now it is twenty-four hour curfew. Very dangerous place; you will not be safe here.'

My heart was sinking fast and my temper was rising. 'But you must help us to get through. We have run the entire length of the Himalayas, we must get through.' I couldn't believe this was happening to me. Not now, surely not now.

The young officer's smile grew broader. 'You must go back and wait until the curfew is over.'

'Well, when is that?' I asked.

'Oh, maybe next week, or month. I do not know.'

'Look, this is crazy. We have full permission from your government and we have run 2,000 miles to get here.' I was angry now and dismayed by what was happening here.

'Well, you better go on then,' said the officer, his smile wider than ever.

'You mean you'll take us through?'

'No, you can go, it is OK.' Beaming.

'But the curfew . . .?'

'No curfew during the day. It was just my little joke.' He fell about laughing and his sergeant cracked up as well.

I turned to Justin. 'We're the best thing that's happened to them all day.'

The soldiers were still doubled up with mirth as we rounded the bend and entered the town itself.

After twenty-eight miles, night-time found us on the outskirts of a village called Awantipur, staying in a café that had been blasted by a Kashmiri bomb during the previous week. Shards of glass and wood splinters littered the outside and the holes in the windows and walls had been hastily covered with bits of plywood. The café sat opposite an ancient Muslim temple which, because it was government owned, was a prime target for the Jammu Kashmir Liberation Front (JKLF).

While we were sitting in the café, a variety of people from the village came to see us: some shopkeepers, an engineer, a student and a revolutionary zealot. The zealot was a JKLF member whose job was in government service. He was still drawing an Indian government wage while fighting for independence. He sat down and started to talk about his cause. His eyes grew wild and soon he was ranting and raving and thumping the table with his fist.

'All Kashmiris will fight. We will struggle and die for our cause. Our leader says that every Kashmiri man, woman and child will lay down their lives for freedom, they will be martyrs for the cause. All the Indian pigs will die and victory will be ours.'

The table-thumping and ranting and raving went on for an hour, with little or no intervention from us. The man worked himself up until the sweat poured off him and his voice grew hoarse. Then, at last, his friends pulled him away and he disappeared into the night, leaving Justin and me feeling extremely uneasy about our situation.

We slept on the hard floor of a tiny room that crawled with flies and as I drifted off, the bomb-shattered windows stared down at me and I felt a real sorrow that such a beautiful place could be marked by such ugliness.

Day Eighty-four. A long, boring road led us into Srinagar, the capital of Kashmir, by ten o'clock. We were going well and for once feeling strong again. 'Strong' of course is used in a relative sense. We had just run for eighty-three days, so 'strong' really means 'just strong enough not to lie down and sleep for a week'.

Srinagar is large and sprawling, full of traffic, soldiers, roadblocks, houseboats on the Daal Lake, hawkers, bustle, noise, hassle and the general hurly-burly of too many people crowded into too small a space. We passed straight through and stopped after twenty-six miles at the village of Narabal.

A small man of fifty-five with a grey beard and laughing eyes and a Muslim cap on his head invited us to stay in his home, where we sat barefoot on straw mats, sipping salted tea and eating chapatis. His twenty-two-year-old son, Abdul Samed Gashroo, spoke excellent English and we spent a fascinating evening talking about religion, politics, marriage and agriculture, and we began to understand the complexity of the current problems in Kashmir as tradition, religion, politics and economics all vie for space in a country sandwiched between the three different cultures of India, China and Pakistan. I learned more from that one night's discussion than I have ever done from reading about the Kashmir situation.

Gulmarg and the finish were only twenty-three miles away.

This was it. Day Eighty-five: the final day and uphill all the way. Gulmarg lay less than a marathon's distance away and 3,000 feet up.

I felt strong and fit and raring to go. I was fulfilling my dream and was running on exhilaration alone. Poor Justin had had the raging trots during the night and was still having to race off into the bushes every few miles.

We ran uphill under a deep blue sky, panting and sweating, past small wooden hut communities, where people stared and smiled at our passing. Up out of the valley, following a silvery grey stream that tumbled back downhill. Then, there it was, far away and high up on a forested ridge, overlooking the valley floor. We knew it was Gulmarg without having to ask. Our minds took over again and we strode out on a high of anticipation.

At Tangmarg, at the foot of the ridge, we quenched our thirst and stared up through the pines towards our goal. Gulmarg, known as the 'meadow of flowers', was an old summer holiday spot in the days of the Raj, and our target was the Christian church that sits in its centre.

Overleaf: A final wash in the Daal Lake by Srinagar

Having satisfied our thirst, we took a deep breath and tackled the final steep slopes. Sunlight filtered through the trees and the only sounds were the rasping of our breath as we climbed, and the soft scrunch of pine needles underfoot. Then, forty minutes later, two tired, sweating but jubilant Himalayan runners topped the rise and ran, panting hard, over the grass and up to the tiny church in the centre of Gulmarg's green meadows.

We had done it!

It's all over

The two of us stood there, huge grins on our faces and tears in our eyes. It was all over at last. We shook hands and at that moment were closer than we had ever been.

The visitors' book in the church was duly signed and then we were both lost in our own thoughts. Not for us the screaming crowds at the finishing tape, nor the slap on the back, nor celebrity treatment. I sat on the grass and stared back over 2,000 miles of the Himalayas and wondered what I had learned. There was a great relief and satisfaction at having achieved the goal and I was terribly proud to have done such a thing.

What an experience this has been!

INDEX